REAL ESTATE FOR REAL PEOPLE

FORMERLY TITLED

REAL WEALTH

REAL ESTATE FOR REAL PEOPLE

WADE B. COOK

Lighthouse Publishing Group, Inc.

Printed in the United States of America

This publication is designed to provide accurate and authoritative information in regard to the subject matter covered. It is sold with the understanding that the publisher is not engaged in rendering legal, accounting, or other professional service. If legal or other expert assistance is required, the services of a competent professional person should be sought. All legal or tax-related information should be verified by a professional.

Cook, Wade B.
Real Estate For Real People
1. Real estate investment. I. Title.
HD1382.5.C67 1990 332.63'24 85-1844

ISBN 0-910019-92-4

Published by Lighthouse Publishing Group, Inc.,
a subsidiary of Wade Cook Financial Corporation
ticker WADE
14675 Interurban Avenue South, Seattle, WA 98168-4664
1-800-706-8657
206-901-3100 (fax)

Printed in the United States of America
Second Edition

10 9 8 7 6 5 4 3 2 1

TO LAURA, MY WIFE

Also by the author
Real Estate Money Machine
How To Pick Up Foreclosures
Cook's Book On Creative Real Estate
In With A Dime Out With A Dollar
(formerly 101 Ways To Buy Real Estate Without Cash)
Owner Financing

Bear Market Baloney
Stock Market Miracles
Wall Street Money Machine

Brilliant Deductions
Don't Set Goals
Blueprints For Success
Wealth 101

Business Buy The Bible

CONTENTS

PREFACE

There are several purposes for this book: to help you understand that you don't have to be trapped; that you don't have to work at a job you don't like; that you don't have to approach the end of each month with no money; that you don't have to face each April 15 with fear or anger; that you don't have to look forward dismally to your retirement years. Another purpose is to share with you ideas about real estate—to put it in a different light—and to show you that it not only answers these dilemmas, but that it can also make many other areas of your life more enjoyable. A final purpose is to give you some basic instruction on how to get started, how to keep going, and then how to retire.

Is real wealth the American Dream? After all, there are many miserable millionaires, and there are many happy poor people. Does money bring happiness? Does the achievement of success bring happiness? If one hundred students sat down for a mid-term essay exam in philosophy, the answers to these questions would be as varied as the clothes they wear. Good answers, all, but varied to the point that for me to suppose that my one answer would fit you would be facetious.

Let me try, though, to put it in financial perspective. Remember, what you do with the money or success is your business. I believe that real wealth is holding a group of assets that continually spin off income so that people can do what they want, when they want to. If you want to be a Boy Scout leader, go do it—the money you need to live on will be in the mailbox on the fifth of every month. If you want to go fishing or golfing, go ahead—your financial affairs will need only minimal attention. Maybe making donations to various charities or working at your church is where you'd like to put your time—if you have real wealth, the money will be there to do it. Perhaps you would like to travel and visit family, or go into politics, or start a new business. Whatever your desire, real wealth is having the means to do it.

When I wrote my first book, *How to Build a Real Estate Money Machine* (now *Real Estate Money Machine*) the publisher didn't want just another get-rich-quick book. He wanted a sensible, attainable approach to making money in real estate. The next natural step was to teach seminars, and this has given me the opportunity to travel to every state and hundreds of cities. My message has been the same. Build up your monthly income. Cut down on the drain of taxes. Prepare for the future by controlling assets that will give you more cash flow when you need it.

Some people think that they can trade being poor for being rich. It doesn't work that way. We trade being poor for being on the road to being rich, and being on the road to being rich is harder than being poor. The risks, the time involved, the decision making requirements, the tension of meeting deadlines and payrolls; all these add up to a challenging life. But if you travel the road successfully and persistently you will reach the pot at the end of the rainbow—whatever that means to you.

Is the trip worth it? I think so because I personally don't like the alternatives. There are many demands on my time, but I vacation when I want to. I go to the office, but I leave when I want to.

Real wealth is having time for your family. Your children need your time. It's having money for lessons and movies. It's having money and time for a special birthday party. I'm not talking about a big chunk of cash, say $1 million in the bank, although that would be nice. Large amounts of cash are hard to come by. And I've sadly found out that when you grow on a cash basis, your tax bracket grows—and this makes it hard to keep growing. There are other assets that grow tax-free, or at least tax-deferred. Real wealth is a cut above just investing for a good return on your money. It's purely and simply having more monthly income because the bills come in each month. How would it feel to have a monthly check to cover not only the bills but also the other things you want to do?

I contend, very strongly, that the way for the average person to "get comfortable" or to "become rich" is by investing in real estate. My radio show "Real Estate for Real People" (which ran for several years on the Associated Press (AP) radio network) was the only such show around. Why does real estate get so little copy? There should be radio reports like this: "Your house went up $72 this week. And, except for a small dip about a year ago, this is the twenty-eighth year in a row that such gains have been made."

In *USA Today* a report was filed on professional sports teams. It said that over half of the teams in the United States were owned by people who had made their money in real estate, and very few of them had anything just a few years before. I'll grant you that many fortunes are made by business people everywhere. I applaud this entrepreneurial spirit. My attempt in this book is to enhance it. If you own a dry-cleaning business or a pet store, read on and see how a little real estate investing will help. Those of you with no money and those who are rich, there's something for you here, too. This is not a bugle call for all to roll up their sleeves and start investing in rundown houses. There are many sensible ways to put your money, or energy, to work in real estate. You pick what menthod will work best for you.

Cash flow makes your investment world go round. The alternative is ugly. Cash flow can be developed, or even created, by following correct principles. There are many ways to build it using real estate.

From my experiences I can unequivocally say that real estate really is the best game in town. There are people everywhere investing: creating income, growth, tax savings, and getting the time to do what they want.

I'm not a CPA, an attorney, or even a real estate broker. I'm an investor. I've never gotten involved in large complexes. I'm just a small property investor who believes in making it big in many small ways. When I originally wrote *Real Wealth*, I used actual examples from my investing and from others I knew. For this updated version of *Real Estate For Real People*, I have not changed the numbers in the examples because the principles remain true. You can reap the same incredible benefits today from these strategies as you could ten years ago. Even though the numbers and prices used in examples have not been changed, the tax laws and timely information has been udpated to be accurate for today.

I can't invest in real estate for you. You have to get up and do it yourself. I can give you the paints and the paint brushes, but the picture you paint will be yours. Obviously, your first attempts won't make it to the Louvre in Paris but, with persistence and tenacity, you'll learn what you need to be successful.

The following chapters will show you different angles to the real estate game; they will show you how to play and win. I hope that you too will find that real estate is the best game in town. Once you put real estate on trial for yourself, you'll realize that real estate stands head and shoulders above other forms of investments.

ACKNOWLEDGMENTS

This book first came out under the title, "Real Wealth." I would like to thank all those who helped update and republish Real Estate For Real People.

First and foremost, I want to thank Catherine Coval, my Real Estate Seminar Director, for skillfully and proficiently reading and evaluating my book. Her insights and input proved invaluable time and time again. Thank you for your encouragement!

Thanks also to Lighthouse Publishing Group: Cheryle Hamilton, Jerry Miller, and Alison Curtis, for your hard work.

Thanks to Mark Engelbrecht, Angie Wilson, Connie Suehiro, Judy Burkhalter, and Brent Magarrell who always work hard to produce high quality books.

Last, but not least, thanks to my beautiful wife Laura, and to my family, who continually support and encourage me.

CHAPTER 1

HOW MONEY IS MADE

How do you make money? Ask ten different investment counselors and you will get ten different answers. How do you save money on taxes, put money away for retirement? Ask the same counselors and again you will get ten different answers. Former President Ronald Reagan said that if you placed all the economists in the world end to end, they would end up pointing in all different directions. Howard Ruff has been one of this country's foremost investment advisors, but he, like so many others, has stated that no newsletter or financial magazine can make people rich. All such advisory services can do is give tips to help people save money, and give strategies to help people put their ideas and their hard work to its best use. There is no clear cut path to financial freedom. Different people have done it in different ways. But, there is a common thread among all of them. And this common thread is not just hard work. If it were, anyone who worked sixty hours a week would be rich.

Many people today who are gaining financial freedom are finding themselves free to enjoy their families and do with their time what they really want to do. In my lectures, I've often said that there are no secrets to success. Success in financial matters, or in a career, involves three points: having a good idea, playing the numbers game, and being persistent. There are some other things that could be done to enhance these three points, but they are basically the thread of success that I see running through most successful people. Let's explore each one of them.

Have A Good Idea

Having a good idea simply means solving a particular problem. The problem can be one that is already ascertained and in the minds of the people, or it can be a new problem that is created for a product or service, and then it is the job of a marketer to make sure that the problem is spotlighted and that the product created to solve the problem fills the need.

Many years ago, I was in charge of a youth organization that sponsored ski trips and dances and other kinds of events for the social well-being of it members. As we were planning events, the questions came up: why is this needed? What are we doing this for? What problem are we solving? What are we trying to accomplish by sponsoring such an event? We were forced to become very "need conscious." If there was a problem, we had to find a solution for it. We had to make sure that the program met the needs of the individuals instead of the individuals meeting the needs of the program. I got so carried away by this way of thinking that if I pulled up to a red light and had to wait too long with no traffic coming from the opposite direction, I would find myself thinking that this light didn't meet the needs of the people.

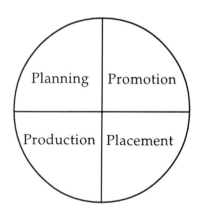

Running a successful business can be compared to the full utilization of the four P's, as diagrammed.

As was so well expressed by Theodore Levill, the goal of being in business is to get and keep solvent customers. Obviously a profit has to be made but the major thrust of the business comes from having customers. Once customers are developed and kept, then the business can be successful year in and year out. Many businesses start out with a great idea. They have a new idea for a toy or for a new computer screen or any other item that can be put on the market today. Without planning properly and ascertaining beforehand the promotion and seeing how well it will work and the costs, nothing happens. If we do not plan and make sure that future demands can be met and all the ideas can be put to use, nothing good can come of it. If the proper planning is done and the production falls down, once again the idea will not come to fruition. If the first three are done–the planning, the production, and the promotion—but then there isn't a good placement system to get the product to market, once again the whole thing comes to a halt. All four P's are necessary to the running of a successful business or successful investment plan. Just having a good idea is not enough, but it is a great start.

Play The Numbers Game

The second point in having success in financial matters is playing the numbers game. I was not the first one to say this. This is discussed in almost every business book ever written. From selling life insurance to selling cars to getting an idea presented before the board of directors all the way to developing a new scientific product, it all starts with playing some kind of numbers game.

We start with the general and we work to the specific. We usually have in mind what we're trying to do, and though many inventions and many new ideas come about as by-products of an original attempt to solve a problem, most ideas are created by having an idea of what is wanted and then going about playing the game until the business people or investors can put it all together to make it work. If it is real estate or some other form of investment, the game is broken down into the looking-and-finding-a-good-deal stage and the holding stage. For instance, if people are looking for the right property, they may have to look at several different houses until they find the one that's going to fit their needs. Let me give a very specific example about this as it relates to the book business. I was learning from one of the largest publishers in the country who said that he received over 3,000 manuscripts a year. Of the 3,000 manuscripts, he would publish about 300. Of the 300 books, 29 to 35 books made a profit, and the other 270 or so would lose money. And of the 30 or so books that made a profit, two or three would become best-sellers and make a large enough profit to offset the losses of the other 270 books. This is the way it is in any business. As people get better in their businesses, as they learn the cycles, as they gain more insights and develop new products, it all comes back to playing the numbers game. The better people get at playing the game, the more likely they are to win. We've all heard the story about Babe Ruth having the most home runs and also the most strike outs; and this part of the chapter can be summed up best when we listen to Thomas Edison's words, spoken after he developed the light bulb. Edison said, "I failed my way to success."

Be Persistent

The third point in being successful and making money is being persistent, as best stated in the following quotation, entitled "Press On," by Calvin Coolidge: "Nothing in the world can take the place of perseverance. Talent will not: nothing is more common than unsuccessful men with talent. Genius will not: unrewarded genius is almost a proverb. Education alone will not: the world is full of educated derelicts. Persistence and determination alone are omnipotent."

Many successful people have had their ups and downs. Their lives resemble a roller coaster. I heard one man say that he almost didn't want to hire any of his key executives unless that person had been through or close to bankruptcy. It seems that the laws of life, the school of hard knocks is the best school around. It is nice to have an education, to bypass many of the mistakes that other people make without such an education. It is necessary, though, to realize the importance of sheer persistence, of having the tenacity to put ideas to work, to try and try again and, if you fail, to get back up and try once more. America was built by people with this entrepreneurial spirit.

There are a lot of new businesses. Each week over 25,000 new businesses are started. Many of these will fail, but those people are not losers and they will bounce back into some other business. Some people might go through three or four different businesses until they find the right mixture or the right idea that is going to make them find their niche and catch on. There are no successful people out there making good money that do not take calculated risks.

Calculated risks come from having knowledge of market conditions or having an inside track. Perhaps it's just having a good idea that is so obvious that everybody will recognize the value of the product or service. I heard a story a while ago of a banquet that was being given for Albert Einstein. Einstein was sitting in the banquet hall next to a young lady and, as they began conversing, she asked him what he did. He said, "I'm engaged in the study of physics." She looked up at him and said, "Oh physics, I studied that last semester." Listen to his comment: "I'm engaged in the study of physics." It's an ongoing struggle to master the science, even for the master.

This idea was well stated by Srully Blotnick when he said, "It's important to become knowledgeable in your own field." The question of how they had succeeded was asked of several hundred people. Now, in a book like this on real estate, you might think that all of them would say that they had made their money in real estate. While many did, this was not the case for everyone. I've asked this same question—how people make it— to audiences around the country, and I get remarks like "they probably made it in the stock market," or "by enjoying what they do," or "by working hard," or "by inheriting or marrying into it." While some of these answers are true, the point is often missed, and it is such a strong point. It is this: the people that made it, that became millionaires, made it by getting to be experts in their fields. One of them, for instance, was an engineer who was making $30,000 to $40,000 a year. After receiving as much formal training as he could, he took additional classes and courses and seminars. He even traveled to take some of these. After making $60,000 to $70,000 a year, and then up to $80,000 and $90,000, he made it rich by socking away a lot of what he was earning. He was living on about $20,000 a year, and he was able to put from $40,000 up to $70,000 a year into savings, and after seven or eight years of hard work, he was "an overnight success" and had become "an instant millionaire." One interesting point is to realize that these people who had made it by getting to be experts in their fields were not necessarily good investors. Their average rate of return was around five to six percent. They were not good at investing; they were just good at what they did.

People could hardly help but be successful if they would take their investing as seriously as they take the training they receive to enhance their knowledge for their careers. It is with the knowledge one has gained up to this day that he will take care of the questions and problems of tomorrow.

The Law Of Leverage

Real estate is a double-edged sword. The rate of return is extremely high because the law of leverage allows you to buy with very little money.

The law of leverage is a means of obtaining an investment with very little money. For example, if one can purchase a property for $100,000 using only $5,000 as a down payment, he has leveraged his money at a 1:20 ratio, or 5%. He now has the benefits of the $100,000 property (growth, tax write offs, and income) but he only put up $5,000. If people get to be experts and know many different angles and different uses for a property, a contract, a mortgage, or any other assets that they are holding, their rate of return can be immensely enhanced because they are not only using the law of leverage, but they are also using the expertise they have gained to make it happen. Like a double-edged sword, they enhance each other and a better investment is made, cash is generated, and more tax write-offs are created.

This next point is true of any business: as we get more familiar with the business and learn the jargon, the ropes, the people, the angles, and the different things that are involved, we get better at making money and therefore have more money to continue growing. We've all heard it said that the first million dollars is the hardest and the second million is a lot easier. This is true. It is true not because the job gets easier but because our ability to do the job gets better.

I can not and will not pretend here that I have the right advice to solve your specific problems. All I can do is to teach as many good principles of investing as I can and hope that you can govern your own affairs in such a way that you will find the success that you are looking for. I do know, though, that we have only so much energy, and we have only so much time to invest. If we find ourselves doing all the work without being able to delegate tasks or delegate certain portions of money to work for us, we will never make it big. Usually the most successful people are the best delegators.

If we do not change our direction, we will end up where we are heading. If you are working at a job that only allows you to buy used Fords and if you don't change your job, you'll be buying used Fords for the rest of your life. I'm not putting down Ford or any other car maker, but I am saying something that has been eloquently expressed by one of my fellow speakers: it's hard to think like a millionaire when you're driving a Honda.

When I heard that expression, I was driving a nice Toyota. I was very content to be a part of the working middle class, and even though I was making good money, I believed that my Toyota portrayed the image I wanted as an investor. Even though I drove a small car like the one I drove when I was out investing, when I am driving and thinking now, I want to be in a really expensive car. So I bought one. I decided that I would play the game to see if it did change my way of thinking. I'm not proposing that everyone run out and buy a Mercedes, but I first bought a Cadillac, and then I bought a Mercedes. I can attest to the fact that it does make a person feel different. Pride alone is not going to get anybody anywhere, but feeling good about yourself and acting the part are so important.

I found myself thinking better thoughts, putting together better ideas, and I almost doubled the gross of my business within a few short months after riding in a bigger, nicer car. I played the part. I felt better about myself and where I was heading.

7

Think wisely. I would be remiss if I said that it does not matter which investment strategy you use. You obviously have to choose the one that feels comfortable for you and one that allows you to take whatever amount of money you have and expand that money into something worthwhile for you. If your funds are extremely limited, then I contend that one of your only form of investment is real estate because it is one of the last bastions in America where a person can go with very little money and make it big. If you are past that stage and are making good money, either from a job or from your investments, and you want to make more money or to preserve those assets that you have already accumulated, then: you need to be buying certain kinds of real estate to maximize what little time you have.

We can talk about having a good idea or about playing the numbers game; we can talk about perseverance, or about any other investment ideas, but none of them work well unless people get excited about them. It is the excitement level that brings about success. Try to show me people who are bored with what they are doing and are successful. I don't think such people exist.

What is it that gets people out of bed a little bit earlier than normal, or keeps them up a little bit later, or drives them to work a little bit harder? It is being excited. If you are not excited about what you are doing now, I suggest you make a change. You not only need to be excited about the effort it is going to take to get there, but also about what it is going to be like when you are there.

I will throw out a caution here. In many cases, being on the road to being rich is a lot harder than being poor. It takes sacrifice. It takes responsibility and commitment, and many people are not cut out for the kind of pressure that the road to being rich necessitates.

But if you're one in a hundred, or if you're just a person who wants to be where you are not, then you are going to need to learn how to make money by using your money and your time wisely—

leveraging it in every way that you possibly can. By keeping up your excitement level so that you can stand the pressures of the valleys, you will find real wealth at the peaks.

CHAPTER 2

NOTHING WORKS UNTIL YOU DO

With any investment, nothing works until you do. Real estate is one step ahead of other investments because once you do work, it's relatively easy to maximize the potential of what little money you have. Once working, you and your money have full support from the law of leverage. With a little practice, you will be compounding the compound effects.

If other people have control of your assets, you cannot command a high rate of return. The closer you watch and manage your money, the better you can expect to do in the business. I wish it were different, but it's not. My theory is to manage my money well now because when it's time to check into the nursing home, I want to own it.

This idea can be taken further. Our investments should take us to a point where we can sit back and enjoy the fruits of our labors. They will if that is our plan and we work that plan to make sure it happens. But don't worry that you will get lazy. When you get to that point, there will still be plenty to do if you want to.

Theodore Roosevelt said, "One of the great American dilemmas is to finally get leisure time and then not know what to do with it." When you have many assets—rental units handled by a property manager, notes, cash, and so on—you'll realize that you have to watch over them. This should not be as time-consuming as acquiring them, but it will take a little time. You'll be there for the beginning, middle, and end of the game. And when everyone else has gone home, the victory will be yours.

You're in charge. You're the one. Nobody else but you will be responsible for your success. You're the quarterback, the locomotive, the chairman of the board.

The real estate kitchen gets busy, heated up, and wild sometimes. Between meals, it's calm and peaceful. But you're the chef, and the kitchen is the only place to cook up good meals. Because so much depends on you, the following points will help you.

Real estate is there for the taking. It's everywhere. If you don't use the leveraging and tax laws to help you, it's your own fault. There are many thousands of people making their fortunes—you can be one of them. Just reach out and buy some properties.

Stay on track. When you find your groove, make it pay. There are three general ways to invest in real estate: the cash out way, the rental way, and the Money Machine way. Find the way that works for you and use it.

A friend of mine bowled in tournaments. He was winning one weekend tournament with only two frames remaining. The prize was $1,000. As he was readying to throw the ball, his contender, an elderly gentleman, walked up and asked him what he was going to do with the prize money. This totally broke his concentration as he started thinking of where he'd spend it. After two frames of Rodney Dangerfield bowling, he lost. It was his, but he lost.

Do not get sidetracked. Success is doing the same thing over and over again. Every other trait can fail. Brains are needed, but there are thousands of unsuccessful geniuses. Contacts are nice, but there are thousands of people who know other people. Luck is great, but there are thousands of individuals whose luck has changed. Persistence, and persistence alone, stands supreme.

Be cautious with adjustments, but be prepared to make them. Use checkpoints. You'll keep on track but will also be keeping your investment on track, solving the problems you set out to solve.

Think big. Only lofty goals raise and inspire men. There is no happiness in mediocrity. Only your big thinking and enthusiasm will keep the others around you working hard. The world truly stands aside for someone with a goal.

Get the support of your family. A very successful basketball coach said, "When a man is about to achieve his goals, it's as if the very forces of nature rise up to oppose him, especially his family." Your family needs to be on your inner team. They're the starting players. Everyone else sits on the bench until you say it's time to play. But your family is on the court with you whether you know it or not.

Tough times don't last, but tough people do.

Make your time count. I know it's hard to stay motivated, but develop some sort of internal motivation. Don't let weeks or months go by without accomplishing something. You're valuable—do valuable things.

One of the greatest advantages of investing in real estate is that you can do only that which you need to do. Many people hear my entire seminar, but very few of them do 100% of what I did. Some do more, but most pick and choose those ideas that they need now. They put to work ideas to solve their immediate problem. As problems change, they choose other ideas.

You need to become an expert quickly. Specialization is the password today.

Good enough just isn't good enough anymore. Do more.

Duplicate. There is only so much time available to us all. One way to maximize that time is to make sure that what we do we can do time and time again. I know this sounds like a tall order, but to simplify it, just think of systems that get the job done.

No two properties are alike. From the beginning to the end, many differences occur, but the system to find them, fix them up, and sell them can be very much the same. I'm convinced that repetition breeds success, even just the repetition of reading the classified section for a half hour or so every morning. Perhaps on a Wednesday, a big deal will be there. It might not be exactly what you were looking for, but perhaps if the terms were changed a little, it could even be better. It's this kind of activity that gives direction to our work.

The statement, made by the president of Wham-O, the makers of Hula Hoops and several other toys, has merit: "I'd rather lose money and know how I lost it than make money and not know how I made it." Can you find in that what I've been trying to say?

If we can duplicate our actions, then we can fine-tune them. If we can fine-tune them, we're on our way to becoming experts.

Guard your cash. In the investing arena your cash is next to your instincts and enthusiasm in importance. If you start solving people's problems with your cash instead of with your creativity, your cash will be gone.

While I was sitting in a laundromat i noticed that the bigger the box of soap people were using, the more soap got poured. Conversely, the smaller the box, the less soap was poured. If you want to buy soap in a bigger size to save money, make sure you transfer it to a smaller box before using it. Or better yet, make sure you measure it each time you add some. Don't use more of your assets unless it's absolutely necessary.

Having cash can go even one step further. Sometimes, just the fact that we have it may make some people feel better (especially bankers). We may not even have to use it. Its existence has built up our credibility enough to swing the deal. Good! Isn't this taking leverage to new heights?

Murphy's Law lurks everywhere. Be on your guard. The only way to beat Murphy is to stay a step ahead of him. Ascertain problems and be ready with answers. Nip problems in the bud by being attentive. Don't get so busy that you let Murphy sneak up on you. I'm not a fatalist; Murphy is beatable, but not if we play on his court.

Part of the purpose of this book is motivational. It's my "Rah, Rah" way of helping people see real estate in all its beauty. It really is like a garden; let it bloom.

This chapter was written for you. I used the word *"work"* in the chapter title because that word is so important. You have to work. Your team has to work. Your offers have to work. The words you use have to work. The properties you invest in have to work. Your plan has to work.

And if all this work can be done at full production, at full capacity, then sit back and watch, you'll not be able to spend all the money you'll make. Investing is done to solve problems. If everything works right, the problems will get solved and you'll have your success, whatever that may be.

Summary

Everything in life is a trade-off. If you do this, you can't do that. If you invest in this, you can't invest in that. The greatest shame of all is that money invested in stocks or metals cannot be invested in real estate.

Real estate produces the benefits that you need to solve your problems. In **Real Estate For Real People**, I've tried to put life back into real estate by putting real estate into life. It will truly do all the good you need it to do.

No other form of investment holds a candle to real estate when all things are considered. It passes the test of time and it's there for the taking.

Get going. Keep progressing. Have fun. And most of all, take control!

CHAPTER 3

AN OLD-FASHIONED LOOK AT REAL ESTATE

Before we get into some of the new ideas for investing in real estate in today's marketplace, we would do well to review some of the traditional concepts and reasons for investing in real estate.

Many books have been written since the late 1940s about the value of real estate investing. As soon as the tax laws changed in the 1950s to favor real estate as a depreciating asset, many more books were written. During this time all the books and all the seminars had as their main theme and thrust for investing in real estate the concept of buying a property and holding onto it forever.

Then other books came along that discussed a faster way to pyramid wealth by buying property and enhancing its value by doing repairs, and then by obtaining bank financing to free up the buyer's cash, taking that money and doing it again with a bigger property. These two ideas were relevant when interest rates were at 4, 5, or 6%. They even worked when interest rates were between 9 and 12%. And though they still work today in certain cases and in certain marketplaces, there are many new ideas that have come about that work better.

The idea was, "look at real estate as a long-term investment." Although I encourage people to do that, there are many other ways of making money today. The long term investment idea worked well and many people started investing when they saw other people making money and when seminars came to town showing them how easy it would be to be rich after X number of years of investing in this way. The seminars and the books of that era shouted out things like: "They aren't making any more of it."

I agree that this is one of the basic reasons for investing in real estate. In the stock market, and even in precious metals, new products can be created. In precious metals there may be a new find that substantially enhances the wealth of the person who owns the mine, but leaves little for the investor. Real estate, on the other hand, is a working person's paradise. When we say that they aren't making any more of it, we literally mean that there is only so much land to go around.

If you own a piece of that land, you have two choices: You can wait, and inflation will raise the value, or a specific event will happen to enhance the value, such as a nearby shopping center or a freeway going through or you can enhance its value by erecting a building on the property. If a building already exists, you can enhance the value even further by expanding or remodeling, or even by tearing the building down and building something new in its place. Real estate investing comes well within the reach of everybody. As a matter of fact, for most people, the primary net asset in their net worth is the home that they are living in. Sometimes when people retire, the only asset that they have built is the equity in their own property.

Owning your own property makes it very easy to make the next move, which is to buy another house. The old idea that if we can do it once, we can do it again, rings true, and once people realized how easy it was to buy real estate, they decided that if they owned a few more pieces of property, they would be a lot better off. Add to this the tax advantages of owning real estate, and it was a natural investment for people of all sorts. Some institutional investors do not want to get involved with the day-to-day buying and renting and repairing that owning property demands. So they invest in trusts and limited partnerships. But for average people, owning a piece of America—as represented by owning their own home—meant that they could do it again.

Many houses, probably as many as 40% of all the houses in America, are lived in by somebody other than the owner. In some neighborhoods, every house is lived in by the present homeowner, but in other neighborhoods every house is a rental property. Of ten houses that are occupied, four are lived in by somebody else, like a renter or a child of the owner. These properties, held for investment purposes, have become the main thrust of many people's fortunes.

When I give seminars, I often ask the question, "How many of you know people who have made it rich in real estate?" Hands go up all over the room. I can almost stop right there and rest my case. It's almost as if real estate is one of the last bastions for the small investor. The theme of this chapter is the theme of the fight song of most real estate seminars.

Furthermore, these seminars and books promote the concept (which I wholeheartedly endorse) that real estate values continually go up. We all know that in any marketplace there can be dips in values. Some places around the country have gone too high in value, and the price is artificially high compared to the cost of building the property. For example, in most cases a builder would buy a lot for $40,000 and build a home for $75,000. He would have $115,000 into the property. He would tack on a fair profit of, say, 10 to 15% and sell the house for $126,500 to $132,250. In some areas of the country, the land may be a little more expensive. The builder pays $50,000 and builds the same $75,000 home, and now he has a $125,000 total into the property. Instead of selling it for $126,500 to $132,250, he can sell it for $137,500 to $143,750. This overpricing has become common in some areas in Southern California and in parts of Texas, Florida, some of the New England states, and even in some of the cities along the Gulf. It is also common in certain neighborhoods in many towns across the country. These are areas that I would not recommend investing in. One of the pitfalls is that people see high-priced homes in nice neighborhoods, and they say to themselves that if they are in real estate, they want to own a home in that neighborhood. And though the adage that real estate has gone up in the past is generally true, it may not be true for every neighborhood.

The caution is to buy and invest where most people are living. If you figure that the average payment in a neighborhood (the average payment that people can afford) is $1,000 to $1,500, then the $100,000 to $150,000 houses are in about the right price range. If you go too much above that, you have just eliminated a big part of the market. You dig for oil where there is oil. It's not only true in the oil business, but it is also true in real estate. You should buy houses where many people want to live; you should not invest in the exclusive areas.

A few years ago a book came out about the crash of real estate. Although there was a lull in the real estate market, it was not caused by the factors the authors wrote about in the book. They mentioned the overabundance causing demand to go down. The demand has always been there. What had happened to cause the slowdown was a high surge in interest rates, making payments so inordinately high that people could not afford to buy. If people have a choice of buying a $60,000 house for $750 a month or renting the $60,000 house for $500 a month, they will rent. Most people are in tune with their pocketbooks and they choose the least expensive way. The book that I mentioned before used a diagram that showed real estate continually going up for the last 1,500 years. I thought it odd that they would use such a blatantly good example as the reason not to invest in real estate.

Should We Rely on Inflation?

If people do not rely on inflation from the economy in general to make money in real estate, they will be very well off. One of the old concepts, though, was to just buy and hold and let inflation do its thing. Many of us have taken advantage of inflation in this way. We have seen the value of our properties go higher than almost any asset that we hold. Couple this with the law of leverage and it's easy to see why real estate has been such a popular subject for books and seminars, and why so many people have become involved. This idea of leverage is an old idea and has some new angles. As long as it works, it puts real estate head and shoulders above any other form of investment.

Every one of these things mentioned still holds true for real estate investing today. Real estate can still be purchased for little or no money down. Real estate is the only form of investment for leveraged tax write-offs. It will continue to grow, and the most important point, as I mentioned before, is that all benefits for real estate ownership can be purchased with cents on the dollar rather than a dollar bill on a dollar. No other form of investment can hold water to real estate because of this one aspect.

As an example, I had a very close friend who was in a jewelry business and was big on selling investment gold and precious stones. He thought I was crazy for investing in real estate because at the time we were conversing, real estate was growing at only 10% a year, and precious metals were growing at about 20% a year. Now, you know as well as I do that these markets fluctuate and you have no control, but ignore this and just stick with the point of leverage. My friend couldn't see why I would take $10,000 and put it into real estate. I let him talk for a while about the beauty of his form of investment because he was really high on it. But he, like so many other people, had totally forgotten about the law of leverage.

We compared the return on an investment of $10,000. He would earn $2,000 at the end of one year by getting a 20% return. I then asked what he thought I could earn with my $10,000. He replied that I would probably earn about $1,000. I said, "Hold it. You have forgotten one thing. I can take my $10,000 and use it as 10% down payment (which I hardly ever do, my average down payment is about 5%) and buy a $100,000 property." Now, if this $100,000 property goes up 10%, that's a $10,000 return compared to his $2,000 return. It took about two weeks for him to get out of the jewelry business and get into making money as a real estate investor. And since that time he has purchased over 40 properties by using a small amount of his cash and borrowing a little bit more to buy others. He now has a net worth over $700,000.

The old ideas are alive and well, but the situation changed dramatically when the interest rates went sky high and banks started putting into the terminology of their contracts a phrase that required that any time a property with a certain type of mortgage was sold, the loan would become due and payable (due on sale clauses). Even if the banks decided not to call the loan due and make the new buyer or the present owner of the property pay off the loan or get new financing, they at least are in control enough to jack up the interest rates and raise the monthly payments—and sometimes to such high levels that people could not afford to own the property anymore.

These changes account for the slowdown in the growth of real estate values. As interest rates came back down and as new programs were developed to circumvent the due-on-sale clause, real estate began to boom once again. But those wise investors who were in real estate before and learned how to roll with the punches and find other ways of investing, and those new people getting involved in real estate who are reading books and attending seminars, will learn new approaches for dealing with banks, and for dealing with sellers of the properties, and even for dealing with tenants on how to collect rents more effectively. Many of these new problems have created one gigantic concern: negative cash flow. At this point I must issue a word of caution about alligators, these negative cash flows.

Negative cash flows are created when the expenses of a property are more than the income. For example: let's say the mortgage payments are $600 and the property rents for $550. There's an immediate negative cash flow of $50 and this doesn't count other possible expenses such as repairs. It also doesn't figure any possible loss of rents from the place sitting vacant. Negative cash flows have been the downfall of many investors.

The questions you must ask yourself are: "How big an alligator can I afford?" and "Do I want one at all?" If you have a property that is losing $150 a month, what is that doing to your investment plan? How many of these can you afford? What are some ways to eliminate the alligators? If they are not taken care of, they have the tendency to destroy any investment program.

Like a rotten orange in a box of oranges, even though it sits there by itself and rots, pretty soon the contamination spreads to the other oranges. And if you don't watch it, the whole box could be contaminated.

This is especially important if you are consistently buying alligators. One bad month, one really hard set of circumstances could come into the picture and totally wipe out all the good that you're trying to do. The following are six tips on how to eliminate alligators, and this process of solving problems can be used for almost any other set of circumstances that could arise:

1. Look to the property. If the property has a negative cash flow, the first thing to do is look to the property itself to see if there are any ways to increase the rents or lower the monthly payments or at least to cut back on the expenses or the fix-up cost. See if the property itself has a solution to the problem.

2. Look to other properties in your portfolio. If there is no way to solve the problem by looking at the property itself, then the next thing to do is to look at other properties that you have to see if the same things can be done there as in the first tip to solve the problems.

3. Look at purchasing other properties. In effect this is going outside your current portfolio to see if there are other properties that you can buy that will solve the problem discussed here, which is a $150 a month negative cash flow. See if you can buy another small property and turn it on contract and get some installment sales payments coming in. See if there is some way of buying another rental unit so that you can create a positive cash flow on that.

4. Look to yourself. See if there is anything you can do by working longer or by working smarter to increase the amount of money you have coming in to offset the negative cash flow.

5. Look to your tax situation. Is there any way that you can increase your monthly income by not paying out in

taxes? For example, if you are able to claim five dependents and are only claiming two, claiming the five might be the exact amount of money you need to cover this negative cash flow and perhaps even others. Are you keeping proper records? Are you doing the right things by taking advantage of all tax benefits allowed to you? These are necessary so that you can keep the money; and even if it doesn't come in until tax time, around April 15, you will have that money available to you to alleviate some of that negative cash flow problem.

6. Look to other people, including bankers and partners. This should be your last source. It is better to go it on your own and solve the problem by yourself, if possible.

Summary

There is a lot of money to be made in real estate. We look back over the history of real estate and see how good it has been for so many people and see it has been bad for so few. There are many points throughout this book on why real estate is good and how to make it good for you. Each one of these points—from leverage to leverage purchases to leverage tax write-offs to control of the measurability of real estate—will be explained in detail. Real estate is a good investment and will continue to be good.

CHAPTER 4

WHAT REAL ESTATE INVESTING IS

There are many more aspects of real estate than meet the eye. It would be nice not to have to include a chapter about making mistakes in this book, but alas, it is necessary, even though there are nowhere near the losses in real estate that there are in other forms of investments.

Although there may not be many huge losses, there are many daily events where any investor has the opportunity of learning and improving. Now, I'm not encouraging deliberate mistakes, only suggesting that living and learning are a part of life. And while you're becoming an expert with your properties, you will also become an expert in real estate, which is the most forgiving investment in the world.

The main reason real estate is so good is that it is repentant. If we want to make a change, we can. If we do something wrong, the procedures are there to make up for what we've done. The result of repentance is to stop a mistake and move on, trying not to make the same mistake again.

You are in control of your real estate investments. If a duplex you own is causing you problems, you can sell it, or evict the tenants—make a change. If you've put too much money into a piece of property, there are many alternatives for getting the money back out. If something isn't quite right, there are professionals waiting to work for you to help solve the problem.

Your personal control is what gives your real estate investments life. I don't recommend doing the daily work: mowing lawns, fixing up, collecting rent, and so on. I do recommend running your investments like a business. Stay near the controls; just get a good co-pilot, navigator, and flight crew to help you.

Just Wait!

It has often been said that if you make a mistake in real estate, just wait. And if the problem doesn't fully correct itself, wait some more. I want to emphasize the importance of this statement because it is true. But even though it's true, I don't want to dwell on it because that may tend to give the idea that I'm suggesting buying at any cost. I do not want to give any such notion.

Many investors have been bailed out of problems with just the appreciation of their property. The forces are in place to help all of us. This idea can be taken even further. Sometimes we stumble onto benefits. Perhaps we've bought a property to create a little income and it just didn't create it this year because the property cost more to fix up than we'd planned. We may even get discouraged. But the next year, on April 15, we realize that we've gained an extra $5,000 deduction for tax purposes.

Then we anxiously await April 15 of the next year so that we can deduct it again, but our tenant makes us a great offer to buy the property. We now realize a handsome profit from our fixing up and can go out and buy some income producers. And just think, we'll probably end up stumbling across more tax write-offs, which will grow in value. This type of problem comes up all the time. Once the property is purchased, the problem turns out to be that it's hard to make a decision. "I know I'm losing $50 a month and should sell it, but I'm saving over $3,000 a year in taxes."

Your Mistakes

We've heard the story that if all the problems in the world were placed in a big pile and we were free to pick, we'd probably take back our own. If you've been there every step of the way as a mistake has occurred, or if suddenly you have a problem with a certain property or your investment plan in general, who better to handle it than yourself?

As most problems develop, we quickly learn the motivations of the people involved. We know to whom to go for help, and because it's our very own problem, we're probably in touch with the details. Sometimes things get really confusing, but there are many professionals available to help us.

Because we have something at stake, we'll quickly formulate a plan to solve the problem. Who is the best baby sitter for our children? That's right—we are. When a rental house burps like a baby, we need to be there. By experience, we'll know what to do to get it back to sleep.

Once again I mention control. You own it. You can solve the problem, sell it, give it away, or anything in between.

Take Advantage

Problems won't go away, but with proper foresight and planning, you can minimize them. It would be a word to the wise to take advantage of these disadvantages.

I've watched people all over the country and have drawn a conclusion from their landlording activities: there are good landlords and bad landlords, and the good ones make a lot of money. Life is too short to be angry and bitter.

At the beginning, I fell into the trap of getting angry at every little thing that went wrong with a rental property. My tenants would call about a broken thermostat and I'd get angry. Then one day I asked myself, "You never get angry like this, why now with these rental problems?" I guess I thought it was someone else's problem. Why should they call me?

Then I noticed the properties of my most demanding tenants. I was taking better care of them and they looked nice. Their values grew faster than did the others. I raised the rent more often. My seemingly "bad" tenants were forcing me to be a good property owner and the extra work was paying off.

Because of this, I changed my whole attitude. Right from the start I told my new tenants that my goal was to make the property grow in value and I needed their help to inform me of anything that was wrong. A few days later one of them called about a leak under the sink. It cost $14 to fix. Can you imagine what it would have cost a few months later when I would have had to spend much more to repair soggy wood?

I hope you get my point. I'm not necessarily recommending that you do the work yourself, only that you see to it that the problems are taken care of. I hired others, including property managers, because one of the mistakes I made was spending too much of my time taking care of these problems—time that I couldn't get back. My time and efforts were not channeled into finding and processing other investments, which is the right thing for the investor to be doing. I corrected the mistake and went on to bigger and better things.

As a matter of fact, it was just these problems (plus having to deal with banks) that forced me to develop the Money Machine concept of turning properties. This concept helped me out of the morass I was in and led me to a lot more money. Today this concept is working for many thousands of others. (To find out more about the millionaire-making money machine, read my *Real Estate Money Machine* or *Wall Street Money Machine* books available at better bookstores everywhere, or call 1-800-872-7411 for more information.)

Necessity is the mother of invention. Necessity and problems will force you to fine-tune your operation, streamline your approaches, and cause you to excel. You'll look back and thank your problems for the solutions that they taught you, solutions that you now use on your other properties.

Time Is Money
There are no classes at the local university to teach you how to be a good investor. You can be taught about deeds and wraparound mortgages and so on, but not about what you should do each day. That knowledge comes by doing it yourself and by learning from the mistakes of others.

I had a friend who watched what I was doing for several months. He asked me one day if he could follow me around for a week to learn all about it. I said okay and he moved into our spare bedroom.

That week was a whirl of activity. Monday there was a staff meeting to set priorities for the properties. After that, I met with a real estate agent to look at ten properties. I made offers on five, and two were accepted on Tuesday. Also on Monday two people called to have me look at their properties. One was being foreclosed on and they just wanted out.

Tuesday morning I finished negotiating on the two properties I had made offers on on Monday. I then went to the attorney's office and closed on one property from the week before. I also bought the one foreclosure and then went to my five-plex to evict one tenant and show a different unit to another couple.

Wednesday I had a meeting with attorneys on an exchange we were trying to put together. I also met that day with another agent on two other properties. These weren't acceptable, but at least he now knew exactly what I wanted.

Thursday was the day to meet with an attorney who was processing sixteen foreclosures. He gave me the files. By that afternoon we had locked up one, and eventually I got five more of them.

Friday I rented two more properties and sold on contract the two properties I had bought on Monday. We then had an office party and took the rest of the day off.

I'll never forget my friend's comment when it was over and we were walking out of the county courthouse after recording documents on six different purchase and sale agreements. He clasped his hands together and said, "Man, I've got to go take some college classes and learn to do this kind of stuff." He missed the whole point. There are no such classes. Success comes by studying and doing, by assimilating information and doing the best you can with the problems you've been given.

Real estate offers us every opportunity in the world for success. We can make mistakes and still come out smelling like a rose.

It Has Controls

Every one of us wants as much security as possible. Yet sometimes we have a tendency to be brazen and make a killing. We're raised with Horatio Alger stories, and each one of us feels that it's our turn to make it.

Wouldn't it be great to find a perfect investment? Don't think for one instant that I think real estate investments are perfect. Far from it. There are risks, hard work, and sometimes setbacks. All I'm saying is, compared to other forms of investments, real estate is the best game in town. One of the reasons this is so is because of the number of controls set up to safeguard real estate values.

I have repeatedly admonished people to stay in control. We all need to invest, but we should invest wisely. There are two ways to make money: work for it ourselves or put what money we do have to work for us. Most people want to get money working for them so that they can slow down or possibly quit working for it physically.

Investing is the only way. If you don't have a lot of excess money, what little you do have you want to subject to as little risk as possible.

It Grows

Steady growth, enhanced by the law of leverage, seems much better than playing wild games. I've already spent enough time on growth and the need for it. I bring it up again here only to make a point.

The growth in real estate may be a little smaller than some other investments, but if we look at the growth on just our cash invested, it's incredible (please refer to the chapter on leverage for more information). That's what we need: good, steady growth.

It Is Steady, With Few Bumps

I would be remiss if I didn't mention that there have been a few slumps in the market. I have mentioned a book that was written several years ago about the real estate crash. I'm not saying that a crash can't happen, but the book was so full of misinterpreted material that I can't believe that it sold at all. The very arguments to refute the authors' claims are right in the book.

The authors used a graph of several hundred years to show a few slumps, but the graph was always going up. Yes, dips in the market appear, but usually in isolated markets. How can anyone use the boom-and-bust period that occurred in Florida during the 1920s to prove anything?

In the past, I've said that some areas of this country were headed for a slowdown in price increases. There was even a need for some price decreases in order to get property values back in line. I've also discouraged people from investing in these areas. Having the general inflation rate of the economy as an only partner is bad business indeed.

Robert J. Bruss, in his book *Effective Real Estate Investing*, puts many of these things in perspective. The so-called real estate crash didn't happen, and if it ever does, most of you, if you will learn the techniques and ideas here, should be retired.

Perhaps, if you look at what happened in real estate a few years, so you could call it a crash if you really stretched your imagination. A recession—yes. High interest rates and industrial downsizing slowed down everything. But like every other setback, it produced a lot of good: there's been a weeding out of the market; the demand is still there—ready for the next cycle, and people's business and their equities have been soaring with new kinds of financing. Many of these innovative ways will help people and investors buy homes for years to come.

It's good to realize that every business has its cycle. If real estate is viewed by itself, you'll see that it fared very well in the last downturn of the economy.

It Has No Yo-Yo Effect

Back to the discussion at hand: controls. If you look at the values of real estate when all of these crises took place, you'll not see a dent. That's the way it is. Do you see people getting appraisals of their property or checking the classifieds every time something adverse happens? Of course not. The values are there. They are values sustained by years of growth—not by some announcement that a foreign country has been invaded, or that IBM is introducing a new computer.

Why are the values so consistent? Perhaps because that's the way we want it. Everyone, of course, has something at stake in keeping values up. Even presidents and congressmen want values to increase steadily. Why do you think so many tax laws favor real estate? We are a nation of landowners. That's good— it keeps the demand high. Another reason may be that real estate can be used for many things: tax write-offs, vacation getaways, rental units for income, retirement growth and income, and so on.

Perhaps the value consistency is due to the MLS computer. MLS, of course, means the Multiple Listing Service found in most real estate offices. Most properties for sale are entered into a computer and all the agents in any given area can access the information. The computer system makes it easy for anyone to see how properties in a neighborhood compare in value to other properties. The computer usually lists the properties that have sold recently so actual figures are given, not some "Pie in the Sky," wishful thinking. The system has not only been a great stabilizing factor but also has created information availability to agents and investors.

This system creates a large network of controls. Appraisals, selling prices, and comparables all show the fact that, in most cases, real estate is measurable. This measurability alone could fill a whole chapter. Let me just say here that accepted yardsticks are in place. These controls almost preclude rapid rises or falls.

We can't forget demand by the average American. Home ownership is not only a dream but also a goal that most people work hard to achieve. Probably more than anything else, this keeps the demand up.

Whatever the reason, you can be certain that if there is a major crisis, your investment will be safeguarded behind these controls. There may be ripples in the market, but steady growth will be there too.

Summary

I'm sure you've realized and thought before about most of what I've been saying. As investors, we need to guard our investments. Our only assurance for survival is to buy low and sell high. That's the American way. What I'm saying is that we need to find good, solid values—wholesale real estate. Then even if there are a few dips, we should be okay. I've dedicated my career as an investment educator to explain this to people who put real estate into life and let it solve problems. The only way we solve problems and not create them is to buy right.

If you will be dedicated to this concept and actually use these smart techniques to help you, your investments will be safe and meaningful, and you will be able to use these controls as a backup system for added safety.

CHAPTER 5

REAL ESTATE IS ATTAINABLE

No plan is any good if the average person cannot do it. Real estate has more passive investors than any other form of investment. Once people gain a certain amount of knowledge, they can find their own niche. Some need cash flow, some need tax write-offs, and others use it as a way to diversify their portfolio. This chapter will help you find yourself and give you the motivation necessary to get things started.

When some people start investing in real estate, for them it is Plan B. These people already have their Plan A going on. They are either working or have their own businesses.

Others have gone out of business and are nearly destitute, and they are looking for another Plan A. They look at multilevel marketing, they look at get-rich-quick schemes, they look at everything. More and more people are settling on real estate. Why? Is it because there are now support groups in existence? Is it because you can buy with nothing down? Is it because someone else did it and made a fortune? Is it because it's down the street? What is it?

Well, obviously it is a combination of all these things. Real Estate is attainable because most people have bought their own home and they can see themselves buying another home. If they can find a deal and if they see it on the way home from work, a lot of people get started investing. But many people say, "That's a good little house over there," not realizing they are going to become real estate investors. All of a sudden they have a property and they say, "That was kind of easy." Then they start looking around for another one. Once you catch the bug, it's easy to get going.

Most people start out with the feeling that real estate is complicated. It takes so much money; it takes so much knowledge; there are lawyers involved and realtors and title companies and who knows who and what else.

But consider the other side of the coin. The sheer fact that all these people are involved is exactly what makes it easy, not difficult. These people are sitting in their offices waiting for you to walk in the door and use them. You don't have to know a thing. You work through a deal with someone to buy his house for such and such, give him so much down now and a little bit later on, and at so much money per month at a certain interest rate and take over his loan. If you don't know how to put it all together, you can go down to the title company the next morning and have them do all of the paperwork.

Who Are You?

When I'm on the road teaching, I have the opportunity to sit and talk with hundreds of people each month, not to mention the thousands that I teach. I constantly hear the same questions asked from Boston to San Diego. The concern is phrased in several ways, but always goes something like this: "Can I still make it? Are all the good deals gone? How do I do more than just make ends meet?" The audiences I speak to are made up mostly of novice investors. But the fact that they are attending a seminar shows me that they are already sold on the benefits of real estate. For a schedule on any upcoming events, please call 1-800-872-7411.

But what about you? Have you been exposed to this information? You probably have to some extent. You've read bits and pieces here and there. You've talked to friends or associates who extol the virtues of real estate but can't help you see the whole picture and, even if they could, can't help you get started.

People today are not only saying, "It's possible," but they're also saying, "I will." Then many fail because the road turns rough, or they weren't fully prepared. Whatever the case, I feel that in today's society and economy, there is no better place to be building a nest egg than in real estate.

The first problem holding people back is money. There is just never enough of it to go around. There are always unexpected things cropping up: medical bills, insurance, losses, weddings, divorces, and, of course, Christmas keeps popping up every year. We borrow, and that creates more problems. We put off some bills, and the phone starts ringing. It's hard to think big with a bill collector at the door.

Where do we turn? Many don't turn at all, they just live a humdrum life. Many save and then see their savings eroded by inflation. Then, in the newspaper or on television, people see an ad on how to make money in real estate. Most people pay no attention, but some find out what it's all about. Of those who do, only a small percentage sign up for or buy whatever seminar or book is being promoted. Of those, only a handful put to use what they've learned. Some of people who begin to invest will eventually be more successful than their instructor!

We've all found ourselves somewhere along this line. Needless to say, the fortunes are made by the doers. If we do nothing, then we'll accomplish nothing. There will never be enough money for as long as we live if we don't go out and get it.

The second problem is taxes. One of the reasons we have so little money is that the IRS takes so much of it. Most Americans spend a good portion of their day working for the government. They don't like it, but most would rather complain about it than put forth the effort to stop it—or at least slow it down.

It's frustrating to pay so much, and then to add insult to injury we end up paying more if we produce more. It's bad enough that we pay more if we make more because taxes are on a percentage basis, but it's really bad that even our percentage increases.

Catch 22? You bet. But there are ways out, and nothing works on taxes like real estate. The chapter on taxes will deal directly and in depth with solutions to this problem. Let me say here that this tax game is just that—a game. But the IRS is for real and plays for keeps.

At the Federal level the game is played for 40% of your income (if you're in the maximum tax bracket), or corresponding percentages for other brackets. State and city taxes are added to this.

Our goal, should we accept it, is to create strategies to keep our money. If we play the game by the rules (their rules) and use all of our resources to do that, then we can keep our money. If we really play well, we can even use what we have created to reduce our tax liability in *other* tax years. For more ideas on reducing your tax liability, look for my book entitled **Brilliant Deductions**, published by Lighthouse Publishing Group, Inc. It's available at better bookstores everywhere.

Many people are not up to playing the game or think that they have to have all kinds of training or money to play. Not so! The rules were created for the average person. All we have to do is play. I have studied (and even indulged in) other forms of investments. Not one holds a candle to real estate when it comes to playing the tax game.

The third problem always pops up when we read Social Security reports or as our retirement years approach. I won't bring up any gloomy statistics here. You've heard them and have been dismayed by them. We all wonder long and hard about the future. After we've been frustrated by a lack of cash flow and the payment of too many taxes, we can find a new dimension to the word *frustration* when we think about our growth. Not only is what little bit we have being eaten up by inflation, but it probably wouldn't have been sufficient anyway.

Think about it. It is one of the most depressing facts of life to know that we're not getting anywhere. It robs those aesthetic aspects mentioned earlier of all sustenance. I have seen people all over the country despair because after all they do, they may still end up depending on Social Security alone.

If real estate is purchased right, there is no better means of growth investment possible. And the great thing is this: the law of leverage. You'll come to realize how you can solve these three problems—cash flow, taxes, and growth for the future—by buying property with very little money out of your pocket. The greatest aspect of all this is that these laws of leverage work to solve all three problems at once.

These three problems won't go away, but neither will all of the knowledge you gain through your experience. That knowledge will give you more confidence all the time. It will help make your goals attainable.

I am reminded of a lecture I once attended in San Francisco about a group of people who had climbed Mount Everest some years before. It was a good presentation because the man speaking had actually been to the top. What I found interesting was how many people started out and how many people actually made it all the way to the summit. There were seven base camps along the way at different altitudes. Two hundred and sixty people started at Base Camp One, including porters, aides, and climbers. There were over sixty climbers wanting to go to the summit. Base Camp Seven was the final camp before the assault on the peak, and about twenty people made it there. From Base Camp Six to Seven, only climbers went. The aides and porters stayed behind.

Then, on a terribly cold morning, with provisions running low and various stages of frostbite found on almost every appendage, six men set out and made it to the top.

I was enthralled by this story of people helping each other, of the perilous cold, and of the hardships they encountered. But

I was more curious as to why only six out of twenty went on. "Who chose the six?" I asked at the end of the talk. The speaker said, "No one. They decided themselves. Each man chose whether he wanted to go or not."

The parallels are obvious. You draw your own conclusions. I didn't meet the other five men, but I believe that they are successful at whatever they are doing because they are winners. Winners don't have to win every battle, only get back up one more time than they're knocked down.

You have within you a winner. Zig Ziglar, a prominent American motivator, gets up in front of an audience and says, "See you at the top." That's an invitation to think like him, to emulate him, to parrot him, to go the extra mile like he does. I've learned by happy experience that great things are only accomplished in the second mile.

You Don't Have To Be Perfect

I don't want to make the various aspects that I have mentioned seem like insurmountable mountains. They are areas that need to be dealt with, though, but remember, every mountain is surmountable. While some readers may get excited, others may get just as frightened. After all, am I not putting all the credit and blame on the individual investor? There are some important points to bring up here to help you.

1. You don't have to learn everything at once. You can learn bits and pieces at a time and use a team of professionals to fill in the gaps. Nobody would make it in this business if he had to know everything. There's not much that you need to know to get started; you only need to know where you want to end up and then figure out how to buy your first properties, and buy right.

2. Real estate investments are only successful for hard workers. There may be some exceptions, but most people reading this book fall into this hard working category. It doesn't take a lot of money or knowledge, just guts and tons of desire.

3. Successful investing in any area requires common sense. Don't think that you don't have any. Most people have an ample amount to get them through, and the closer you get to your own pocketbook, the stronger your common sense becomes.

   Let me give you an example of common sense at work. Many people do not realize how easy it is to find good deals. Once you start the process and play the numbers game to its fullest, excellent opportunities will present themselves. At first, you'll want to get them all, and you'll probably take on more than you can handle. Then it will dawn on you that you're overextended. You need to cut back. Eventually you'll find the happy medium and be processing the right number and types of properties.

   It's almost cruel to say that too many people go through these pangs of growth: one period doing too much and then a few months later doing too little.

4. Problems will not go away and neither will opportunity. You will grow and change, and the knowledge and experience you've gained until today will answer the questions and solve the problems you encounter tomorrow.

5. The ups and downs of our needs require us to set up "Checkpoint Charlies" along the way. Not being perfect, we need to see how we're doing. Let's say we set a goal to buy six properties this year. They need to be in the $100,000 to $120,000 price range, with one or two way below that, if possible. We need to cash out of one property to free up $20,000 to $30,000. Two need to be turned on the Money Machine concept to generate some monthly cash income and avoid huge tax liabilities by claiming our gain on the installment sales method. (See *Real Estate Money Machine* for these powerful strategies. Call 1-800-872-7411.) Three of the six need to be good rental properties, with low or nothing down, break even or positive cash flow, and be in fairly good neighborhoods.

If all this is accomplished, this year we'll be sitting pretty, but we can't wait until Christmas to figure out how we're doing. We need monthly evaluations, and we definitely need a major midyear evaluation and reevaluation session. It's too easy to get off course if our goals stay the same and too easy to stay on course if our goals change. Sometimes we need to change and amend our goals, direction, and emphasis.

This reevaluation aspect is important. No business can get along without it. The alternative to continually checking our progress is to flounder, getting into deals that aren't right, selling at the wrong time, buying for the wrong reasons, and so on. I call these times "Checkpoint Charlies." They are exciting because change is exciting. Here's a little format I use that you may find helpful:

Step one: Restate the original goal and the rea son behind it.

Step two: Evaluate your progress. Be specific.

Step three: Reconsider your goal and the reasons for it to see whether or not it is still valid.

Step four: Rewrite a new goal and the reasons for it (if it is the same, that's fine too).

Step five: List the actual things that you'll need to accomplish to reach your goal. Once again, be specific.

Step six: Ask yourself this question: "What else could I be doing with my time and money?"

Now, review your findings, your new goal, and your intended actions in the light of this last question. This is "Checkpoint Charlie," and if it is ingrained into your affairs, it will become a valuable tool that you'll use every day. You don't have to be perfect if you know how to effectively amend your plan and keep heading toward your goal. You'll find your goal more attainable than ever before if you incorporate this checklist.

6. You can start anywhere and use the knowledge you've gained elsewhere to help you. Every one of us has been doing something, and in almost every job that I can think of, there are certain aspects that, with a few adjustments, can apply to the corresponding aspect of real estate investments. Perhaps you are selling something, or running an office, or doing carpentry. Perhaps you're a doctor, with patients and time schedules, or you're a politician, or whatever. Something you're presently doing can and will become a real asset to you.

You may not be a full-time investor, but you can get going on something. Perfection is acquired, not inherited. Doesn't that make you feel better? Progress toward perfection is the key, and looking for a more excellent way of doing things is a daily challenge.

Leverage

I will spend a whole chapter on this subject (Chapter 6), but let's mention it here now so that we can put it to work in the light of attaining your goals.

We take what we have—our talents, our energy, our money, our needs, our ability to work with others—and we put them to work for us. Each of us has enough to get started because it doesn't take much. We can leverage each one of the attributes if only we'll start the process. Then the natural leverage growth and income aspects take over and we're off and running.

Remember, though, that no one else can or will do it for you. We're forced to take what we have—imperfect though it may be—and make the most of it.

Summary

This chapter has been written to give encouragement to you to get going and start the process. However, I do not want to minimize the necessity of being an expert.

We can start on our own and surround ourselves with good people, but if we're not moving forward toward being an expert in some aspect of our investments, then we're missing out on a great opportunity.

Every day you'll have opportunities to get better at what you're doing. You can get better at one small thing by doing it over and over again, and this will help your whole investment system. Because real estate is varied, it's exciting; and because it's exciting, it's fun to grow and achieve.

In the whole array of real estate investments in which you can be an expert, you need to pick one and then become a specialist. We all know that the specialists are taking over the world. It's right and important that we find our area and concentrate on it.

I've been asked many times, "What do I do first? Where do I start?" These are important questions with important ramifications. Let me answer by restating the questions differently and then answering the new question.

"What can I do that will mean the most to me in the long run?" I like that question because the answer to it will help us see things more clearly. *I will answer the question simply by saying that no area of expertise will mean more in the long run than developing the ability to find value.* Finding the properties (or any investment) that have the most built-in equity or potential of easily creating this equity has meant more to all successful investors than any other element.

I'm not concerned here with the reasons for investing, but with the actual investment itself. Some people get to be experts in tax shelters, or in writing offers. Others specialize in landlording or in developing. All of these are important, but none of them make sense if the value is not there.

Find the value and all else will happen naturally. I see investors buying rotten deals because they're good tax shelters. I see others spinning their wheels trying to be a master of negotiating. If they would just stop and look at what is important, they would change their actions. Instead, they would play the numbers game to find good solid value and let all these other great aspects fall into line.

No other form of investment lets the small investor capitalize on finding value as real estate does. People will always be in trouble and need to sell quickly. There will always be foreclosures and rundown properties. They are on every block; we drive past them on the way to work.

It's just a matter of making the deal click that is left up to you. I know from my experiences and from those of thousands of others that almost all of our emphasis should be put on buying low and selling just below high. I've tried other ways, and they don't work.

It would be hard to list all of the various aspects in order of importance. That will depend on you, but I will state the area that I think is second in importance. It is the structuring of our purchase offers. Our goal is to keep all of our doors open so that when it's time to sell, we're ready to go. It is important to write up the offer to allow this to happen. As a matter of fact, one of the things that adds a lot of value to the property is the right to write up our own purchase offers. There we are again: back to value. These two ideas go hand in hand. We find the right property, and we write it up (purchase it) in a way that lets us capitalize on all of its equity and potential.

The other areas (taxes, growth, landlording, and developing) need emphasis also, but your job in these areas will be so much easier if the transaction is right to begin with.

CHAPTER 6

LEVERAGE

Most people don't understand the law of leverage as it affects real estate. They may know a few things about it, things such as that leverage is OPM (other people's money) or some similar definition. Therefore, the many other characteristics of real estate leverage are not realized and used.

The simple fact is that most of us don't have any money; those of us who do have some need to be very cautious about spending it. Leverage to me means letting a little do a lot. There probably isn't an aspect of real estate that gets so much exposure with so little deep thought.

We are in the leverage age. We need to get the most out of everything we do. When we invest, we need to get the most from our money. It must work hard for us, and the best way to do this is to make sure that what little money we have controls property the best it possibly can.

If we can tie up and control a $200,000 eight-plex with only $5,000, the results are incredible. We'll get the growth and income and will also get the tax write-offs. If the same purchase required no down payment, then the rate of return would be infinite—it can't be measured.

If such an event just happened once in a while, I wouldn't even mention it here. But the fact is that it's happening all over the country in thousands of transactions every day.

Leverage is like a seed. You've heard the one about the acorn that grows into the mighty oak tree. In real estate our seed is leverage, and it's just waiting to be planted.

Benefits

In another book, **Real Estate Money Machine** Visit your local bookstore and get a copy and call 1-800-872-7411. I mention selling the benefits rather than the features of a property. Features stick with a product (or idea) whether you buy it or not. Benefits, however, can only be derived if you buy and use the product or idea. So it is with leverage. The law is simple and just waiting for us to use it.

Putting It To Work

How do we take advantage of this great law? Consider the following seven points:

1. There are many properties out there that can be pur-
    chased with little or no money down. It may not seem
    so at first because they don't stick out. You have to dig
    in and find them. Perhaps your home town doesn't
    have many opportunities, but there are communities
    all over this country with many good deals.

2. When you start the negotiation, agree to pay cash only
    as a last resort. Don't tell the sellers you have any
    money or tell them you need it for the fixing up. Per-
    haps you can tell them (and ease their fears about you
    at the same time) that your successes have brought on
    a tax liability and you need your money for that; you
    need their property for a tax write-off.

3. There are advantages for your selling other than the
    cash advantage, and these same advantages are avail-
    able to them. Educate them about these aspects of
    selling.

4. There are ways to get them cash without the cash being
    yours. Many books have been written on this, includ-
    ing my book entitled **101 Ways to Buy Real Estate
    Without Cash,** available at better bookstores every-
    where. Familiarize yourself with these techniques.

5. Be very concerned with the cash flow situation of the professionals around you. Remember, however, that many of them are willing to take their fees down the road or with monthly payments. As a matter of fact, many of them relish the opportunity. They see themselves getting into deals that never existed before and wouldn't exist without their willingness to take their commissions and fees this way (please see Chapter 4, "My Real Estate Agent Loves Me," in *Cook's Book on Creative Real Estate* available in better bookstores everywhere.

6. Leverage extends to other areas also. For example, what about a book that you buy for $20, which gives you one idea that earns you $8,000? Or a $200 seminar that shows you fourteen new concepts for problem solving—your income or savings this year could be $10,000, not to mention the next umpteen years of continued money making.

7. Using very little of your own money allows you to move on several properties at once. This may be mandatory if you need many purchases for tax savings.

Putting It All Together

Let me tell you about my friend the locksmith. I was in the habit of changing the locks on every property I bought (my locksmith would go out and do it for me as he was servicing other clients). We had many opportunities to talk. He was tired of his 14 hour-a-day business, and after watching me get into and out of so many properties, he made his first brave move. When I went to his shop one day, he ran up to tell me of the duplex he had bought in the south part of town. It was in a good neighborhood, and he bought it for only $50,000. He was excited because he only had to pay $12,000 down. I didn't want to burst his bubble, but I said, "Doug, I think we'd better have a talk."

We spent an hour or so discussing the law of leverage. $12,000 was way out of line. He thought he was stuck with it but decided he'd go back and try to negotiate the purchase arrangements. Luckily for him, they thought a note would be just fine if he would agree to pay their original asking price of $52,500. He did and only had to tie up $1,200 of his money.

Armed with this new information and excited about purchasing more, he used the balance of his cash and purchased six more houses in the next six weeks.

Now, he had the best of all worlds. The laws of leverage that make the purchases click are the same laws that make the other aspects of real estate soar. What if an investor's $1,200 can produce $50 of monthly income, $5,000 of equity, and a $4,000 tax write-off to boot?

The leverage law is one law with many great effects. I do not understand how people can invest any of their hard-earned cash on any investment that doesn't maximize the laws of leverage, and most investments don't use even an ounce of leverage.

In this investment economy, one of the things I teach is the principle of not trading cash for equity. It's not a fair trade—not my hard-earned cash for someone else's equity. If I have to put in any cash at all, it must meet these three requirements:

1. It is not a large amount. It's hard to say what is a correct amount because there is no right or wrong, just varying degrees of effectiveness. Your main objective should be to look for value. Once found, you need to get in light so you can get out light. This concept has helped more people than I can count. It lets you sell easily. It keeps the balance of your cash free to do other things.

2. It has purchase-potential. Once again, value is the key. I've often seen people buy houses at market value with too much down. Yes, they'll get the income, growth, and tax write-offs, but not as much as they could if they had searched out and bargained for a better opportunity. When I have to put in cash, I must purchase a lot of potential. What kind of potential? Cosmetic work, cleanup, raising the rents, and so on— anything that will increase the value without devouring much more money.

3. I can easily get my cash out. (My rate of return on the rents must be high or I'll need to sell it). I'll only put my cash in if the property will sell quickly. For example, I found a house worth about $50,000 to $52,000 ($60,000 if fixed up fit for a king). It needed a lot of minor repairs, but it was vacant and being foreclosed on with outstanding loans of $20,000. Great deal so far, but there was $4,000 in back payments.

I wanted it and had to scrape to come up with the $4,000, and even at that I was worried about the $1,000 I'd need to clean it up and repair it. But I did raise the $4,000. Now, some people will say that this is too much down. Maybe it is, if we look only at the price, but if we look at the value and the amount of equity that will be immediately created, it will be a great buy.

I bought it and then didn't have the $1,000 to fix it up. But a young engineer and his wife wanted it because it was close to Boeing, where he worked. They gave me $1,000 as part of a $6,000 down payment, with a purchase price of $50,000. They didn't have the time to fix it up and wanted me to use their $1,000 to do it their way. I gladly obliged. A week later they paid the balance of the $6,000, and I was able to cover the checks I had written. Sometimes we do things by the skin of our teeth when opportunity knocks.

In short, I want my money working for me again and again. The only deals I'll get involved in have a revolving door like this one. And think about it: how many times a month can you do something like this?

Leveraging Ideas

This brings up the next point. Think how important it is to our sanity if we can get good at just a few things, hire professionals to do the rest, and capitalize on these ideas over and over again.

Repetition breeds success—we don't need a hundred ideas. All we need is one that works. If we're specifically using leverage to buy, all we need is one system, one formula, one technique that gets us in.

It's comforting to know that we don't have to know every-thing there is to know about real estate before we start taking advantage of it. It's also comforting to know that the law of leverage is available for leveraging ideas. It's also available for leveraging one other area: people.

Leveraging People

Leveraging money and ideas takes on new dimensions when we realize that we can also leverage people. We can make them rich (agents, and others) if they will put our ideas and money to work.

It's also leverage for them. Just think, real estate agents need us as much as we need them. They can take our money and, if invested wisely, create an immediate commission and client. If they do a good job, the client relationship goes beyond the immediate and on to other transactions.

If our time is taken up elsewhere and we have very little left for actually doing the footwork, then we can leverage a few hours to educate someone to work for us. This aspect just makes everything else better. There is a whole chapter on this subject coming up.

And It Gets Better

Once the ball starts rolling, more opportunities arise for getting into other properties. Think of the leverage created after a few years on even just a few properties. The equity can be used for generating cash or for trading. Most likely the rents will be going up. These rents create more cash and value with every increase. If the property is sold on installment or with a balloon note due later, this equity note can be used for other things. A balloon payment or note is an amount due which is larger than normal. For example, a $20,000 loan is due with $200 payments. If left to amortize it may take 12 years to pay off (depending on the interest rate being charged) but if the unpaid balance be-comes totally due and payable in five years it is a balloon payment.

Leverage

Let me give a scenario of what could happen. You buy a fixer upper for $45,000 and use $4,000 for your down payment and fix-up costs. You rent it a year or so. The value has increased to $67,000 because of fix-up and inflation in general. The cash flow has been on a break-even basis. Now you sell it for $65,000 (a little under market so that it will sell quickly) on a wraparound note (see chapter 10). The down payment to you is $6,000.

You now have your original $4,000 back, plus an additional $2,000. You decide $4,000 is all you'll need right now for your next round of investments, so you take a trip to the Bahamas with the extra $2,000. When you get back, you go buy another property and repeat the process.

In the meantime, your equity note is now producing income with very few tax liabilities. Your equity note is $17,000. This is figured by taking your receivable note of $59,000 ($65,000 minus the $6,000 down payment) and subtracting your payable note of $42,000 ($45,000 purchase price minus the down payment of $4,000—the other $1,000 was the fix-up money.) The net cash flow on this is now $150 per month. This is figured by taking the $600 payment on the $59,000 note coming in minus the $450 payment on the $42,000 note going out.

You could just sit and ride with the payments, or you could use them another way. You could discount and sell the note and mortgage. You could borrow against it or even trade it into something else.

The important thing here is this: the note is leverage at its best. It cost us nothing to create except our time and energy. We have our original cash investment back so that we can reinvest it. We have all these opportunities for future leveraged growth, and we got a trip to the Bahamas out of the deal.

Can you imagine how this deal could be enhanced if we could get money back at closing on the purchase of the property? All of these things happen every day, and I enjoy getting letters with people's success stories and questions.

Existing Loans

One of the easiest forms of leverage is assuming existing loans. Remember, don't think of leverage just in terms of money, but also in terms of your time. The most successful single family home investors are experts at assuming loans—especially old Federal Housing Administration (FHA) loans.

Let's look at the following twelve aspects of assuming FHA loans, and you'll wonder why you would want to do anything else:

1. They're fully assumable.

2. There is no qualifying for pre-1989 FHA loans. However, there is a name-change fee.

3. They don't have to be owner-occupied. There is no limit to the number you can assume and hold at one time.

4. You don't even have to have a pulse rate! You can be a corporation or even a bank.

5. It can be assumed from you; then again and again—no limit.

6. It can be "wrapped" as many times as you like (see Chapter 10).

7. The interest rate will never change.

8. The monthly payment doesn't change (unless it's one of the few loan types that have increasing annual payments).

9. Mortgage holders (banks) don't call the loan due or change any of the terms.

10. If there are existing second and third mortgages, mortgage holders (banks) won't call them, because if they did, they'd have to pay off the first mortgage or assume it, which they won't do.

11. They usually have lower than average monthly payments and interest rates.

12. The house, no matter what condition it is in now, at least met some kind of standard before the loan was made.

All in all, it is a perfect loan to track down. Think of the effect your time and money will have with these. Yes, they may be more scarce now, but they are out there. And think of the alternatives— two weeks can be spent dealing with one banker over a due-on-sale clause, or finding one good old loan.

However, keep this in mind: pre-1989 FHA loans are few and far between and balances will be very low because of their age! Focus on Adjustable Rate Loans (ARMs)—almost all are assumable—with qualifying.

Partners, Options, and Others

I would be remiss if I didn't point out a few other ideas. Using other people's money is a key. The easiest and most logical source of funds is the seller, but there are other places. One is banks. Very seldom is the return or growth on a good property less than the interest and financing charges that you'll pay a bank.

Partners can be taken on to invest the cash needed for the down payments and to handle any negative cash flow that may be created.

If you're serious about your abilities and feel that taking on some limited partners may be the answer to your problem, then I highly recommend a book by Greg James called *The Power of Real Estate Syndication*. The book has a great deal of useful information. It's easy to understand and yet highly technical. It's good not just for real estate, but for any endeavor for which you may need money. Partnerships may allow you to put to work some of the great ideas of real estate.

Options to buy real estate are another source of leverage. You can tie up a property without ever owning it. Usually this requires very little money for the option payment. You can get the benefits of real estate without ownership. Ken Otterman's book *Real Estate Investing for Cash Flow* covers this and many other ways to use real estate to create cash flow.

Donations

Most of our ideas are worth a lot of money. How about taking these ideas or at least the money made from them and giving them to your favorite charity? Leveraged real estate makes this possible. Now, you may give away anything you have no matter what the cost, but if you can give away an equity note that cost you nothing to create, it could help solve other problems as well.

Let's take the note mentioned in the previous example and give it to a charity. Donating it lets us deduct the full $17,000 from our gross income. This donation backs us down through several tax brackets, and we can now pay $6,000 less in taxes. Now start measuring your rate of return.

It's amazing the good we can do in the world and write it off at the same time. Most of us want to do this but just don't have enough money. I'm reminded of a story about Brother Brown sitting in the congregation of his church. The reverend says, "Brother Brown, if you had two big houses sitting on a hill, would you give the church one?"

Brother Brown says, "You know if I had two houses I would give one."

"And Brother Brown, if you had two big Cadillacs, would you give one to the church?"

Again he says, "You know I'd give you one of those Cadillacs."

"Brother Brown, if you had two white shirts, would you give the church one?"

"Now, wait a minute, reverend. You *know* I have two white shirts!"

It's easy to give away in thought what we don't have. Henry Ford said that you can never give anything away—it always comes back. No one can measure the amount of good the Ford

Foundation has done. Leverage and real estate working together just make it better for everyone, even the IRS, because charitable donations take the strain off the government. By doing things right, we can not only give a little but also give a lot.

At Risk

When putting any investment on trial, we look at the risk. It's necessary to understand what we can lose. There is a slight possibility that we can lose with real estate. Maybe one out of 400 transactions turns bad. But what we lose if we don't invest in real estate is not only the profits, but also the right to "lose" more than we actually have "at risk."

With real estate you could put little or nothing down and create huge artificial tax losses. Think of it, you could make $5,000 cash on one property and actually have a net loss for your tax return—paper losses let you pocket profits at their best.

Summary

All of these ideas and advantages set real estate apart from every other form of investment. Leverage lets you transform your ideas into realities.

CHAPTER 7

INCOME GENERATION

It is probably safe to say that we all need, or at least want, more income. There is never enough at the end of the month to meet our demands. This is not just a recent problem, but one we've all faced in different ways. Making income compatible with outgo turns our thinking inside out.

We've all handled this problem in our own ways. There were only two things that could be done: make more or spend less. Some of us have taken part-time jobs. Many others have taken additional educational courses to qualify for higher positions with more pay. Others have just finally asked for a raise.

On the other side of the coin, many people have chosen to spend less. They've moved into less expensive living quarters. They've put off going on vacations, buying clothing, and eating at nice restaurants. To some, spending less has become a way of life.

Most of us have done a combination of these things because we've been forced to. Sometimes we do it because we want to create more income for other things. However, most of us just don't make enough, especially in light of what inflation has done to our money.

We only have so much time, and most people have committed their working time to the maximum. Making money is time-consuming, and making that extra amount to get ahead is sometimes too much. There are no more hours in a day, and even if there were, there's not much more energy to go around.

Let me list here some "facts" that I've discovered as I've talked with people:

- Everyone wants to get ahead. Many want to quit their jobs, and the ones who enjoy their jobs still want more income so that they can enjoy other areas of their lives more.

- Most people realize that while lots of cash is nice, creating a steady monthly income will mean more in the long run.

- Most people realize that gradually creating enough steady income to quit a job or work less is easier than finding the cash necessary to do the same all at once.

- Most people realize that if it is only their long, hard hours that will bring them financial security, they're really hurting. They also know that it will take putting their money to work to get them ahead. Once these facts are thought through, many people realize that it doesn't take much money and it doesn't matter whose money it is to leverage financial security.

Now, that brings us back to you. Are you willing to pay the price? I've often said, "If you'll do for a few years what most people *won't* do, you'll be able to do for the rest of your life what most people *can't* do." I want you to know that I'm biased. I've spent the last seventeen years writing and talking about cash flow. I've seen problems in my life and in the lives of many others because emphasis was placed on some other area. I mention finding value because of the cash flow it can generate. I bring up tax savings because of the cash flow investments it can create, not to mention the immediate cash savings. When I talk about equity growth, my main concern is the cash flow it will generate in the future.

Many people have said that the three most important things about investing are "location, location, location." I don't want to throw this idea away, only put it on a back burner. Today I contend that the three most important things about investing are "cash flow, cash flow, cash flow." If you question this, look at the alternatives. All the alternatives to cash flow are gruesome. Cash flow makes your investment world go around. Without it, everything else comes to a stop.

I'm not saying anything to diminish the importance of any other aspect of real estate investing. I'm just saying that cash flow must be given top priority. Once it's created, you can do almost anything.

Income For The Present And Future

We need this income for the present. It allows us to pay the bills, and perhaps quit our jobs. It also allows us to invest for our future.

There are many ways to create income, but none as good as real estate. The primary reason for this is the great old law of leverage. Not one of us would have the cash necessary to buy the investments we need to produce the income we need if we had to pay one hundred cents on the dollar for that investment.

Leverage allows us to buy more properties, and whatever rate of return we can get is magnified if we tie up very little money.

Kinds Of Income

There are five kinds of income generated by investing in real estate. The first is rental income. If we're willing to play the landlording game and maximize our time and money, we can generate a lot of rental income.

The second is tax income. Sometimes we have to forego making a positive net monthly income, but more often than not, this will have a great effect on our tax situation. If we work it right, we could even have less withheld each month so that we can pick up more monthly income this way. And, if not this year, then we'll get it back after we file our return next year.

The third type of income is from notes. Almost everyone who has been investing for a while will have some kind of notes receivable. These come into existence by taking one's equity in the form of monthly payments instead of cash. Later in this chapter, I'll discuss several ways to get this going, and you will find a full explanation in the chapter on the Money Machine concept.

The fourth type of income is not too common. It is income derived from fees or commissions you may receive for investing other people's money.

The fifth type of income is created when you sell the property (your equity) for cash. Your buyer either gets a loan, or pays you from his own funds. You're now out of the picture on this property if you get all cash, but you do have the cash.

There are combinations of these types of income. You may rent for a while and take in the rental income, all the while saving on your taxes. When the time is right to do so, you may sell for a lot of cash down and carry a small mortgage. The possibilities are numerous.

Rental Units

For years this has been the primary focus of all real estate investing. People from all walks of life hold billions of dollars of rental units. The value of real estate has gone up and remained high because so many people want it for so many reasons.

Everyone thought that you had to hang on forever because the property would grow and become the source of retirement income later on. Hundreds of books have been written extolling the virtues of, and showing people how to get in, stay in, and retire from, these rental properties.

Although I have some problems with this concept (which I'll list later), in theory the premise is right: properties do produce rental income and at the same time spin off tax shelters while growing in value. Because of this, everyone has done what they could to maximize the income and minimize the work while holding these properties. "Raise the rents—lower the expense" has been the theme song, and some of the cleverest things imaginable have been thought of and tried.

I heartily endorse this concept once investors create cash flow enough to solve their other problems, but in today's economy I don't think purchasing rental units is the best answer at first. There are other alternatives for the beginner.

I really don't want to be misunderstood on this point. Rental units are great, but for the novices or even for those investors who have not yet created enough income, all the aspects of real estate investing will be better if they will put their emphasis elsewhere.

I'll list several points to consider here and then immediately give the solution to the problem as I see it:

My first concern is that most of us have to save for quite a while to buy our first property. Yes, property can be purchased with no cash, but more often than not it requires a little cash. Even if it's only $1,200 to $1,500, our money is gone. It will take a while to dig up that amount again. So, whether the property breaks even or makes $50 a month, the down payment is gone.

I can't begin to count the number of people who have put too much into a piece of property. Once their money is gone, they're back to the waiting game—out of control. They know they can find other good deals, and they have the energy and desire to find them, but they do not have the money.

I'm reminded of the man complaining about his day on the golf course. "What a rotten day! I kept hitting the ball into the water or into the sand trap. And then my golfing partner Fred died on the eighth hole. There I was the rest of the day—hit the ball, drag Fred, hit the ball, drag Fred."

It's not uncommon to feel this way about our investments if we put in too much money. I just don't believe in trading cash for equity on a long-term basis. I want it back out to go to work again.

The second major concern I have with rental units for the small investor is the inordinate amount of time that rental properties absorb. They can take up any free evening because there's always something that needs to be done.

The problem gets worse when you think of the trade-off. Everything in life is a trade-off. If you go to the beach, you can't go to the mountains. If you spend your time tracking down a tenant to collect the rent, you can't be out finding the one great deal that may let you stop working in someone else's business.

Investing in real estate can be a business for you and you will be successful if, and only if, your time is spent on priority items. You need to prioritize your time and realize how valuable you are.

My third concern is the emotional strain of dealing with tenants. They don't own the property—you do, and they'll never treat your property the way you want it to be treated.

I heard a joke a few years ago about a tenant sharing a unit with two other tenants. He finally went to the authorities complaining that Bill had twelve dogs and never let them outside. He wanted relief because he couldn't stand the smell or the mess. The official asked: "Why don't you open the windows for some fresh air?" He replied, "What, and let all my pigeons out?"

The obvious solution to this problem is to hire professional management people to alleviate the problem. This is a good solution after you have cash flow built up.

The fourth point that concerns me is that it always costs more to own a property than originally anticipated. There are hundreds of things that can go wrong, which, if only a few actually occurred, would cost a lot of money.

Very seldom does Murphy stay in his closet. Rents don't come in and expenses don't stay down. These costs can kill any investment plan. Caution and wise planning are the keys. There really is a time and place for everything. New investors usually don't need tax write-offs, so rental properties may not be needed at first. Besides, there is a better way.

I think it's about time to give the solution. I haven't wanted to put you off, but only to have you feel my frustrations. The solution is to sell the property. I'm not talking about selling to create more problems, but selling to solve problems. You sell to create steady monthly income.

If such a move requires a bank or savings and loan, you may run into other problems. When you sell, I think the easiest way to generate the sale without problems is to not chase after cash. If it comes chasing you, take it, but don't get tied up with all the problems of chasing it.

What I'm talking about here is the Money Machine concept of investing in properties. It's a tried and proven system that works all over the country in all kinds of communities that have a good economy (no investment plan works in depressed areas). I developed the system from the ideas of others. Back in the 1970s when everything turned to gold in the Midas Real Estate Era, any plan worked—dealing with banks, having tenants, and so on, it didn't matter. Money was cheap and rents were high—just invest and sit back.

To say that times have changed would be an understatement. We need new ideas, new plans, and new systems. Our goals haven't changed. Our needs haven't changed, but the way we handle them has to change with the changing economy.

People investing the old way can get hurt. I did and I got hurt. I developed a different system, and in my own way I have tried to teach this concept to as many people as would listen. I've not just tried to put life back into real estate, but put real estate into life. I firmly believe that, if handled properly, there still is no better game in town. Real estate can solve our financial problems if we remember to do things in their own proper order.

The equity growth on these Money Machine properties was great. The monthly income was greater, and if you'll read the tax chapter, you'll be sold on this plan when you realize how small your tax liability will be when you sell this way.

Even if you do it once in a while to create a little more income or to help offset a negative cash flow on another property, or even to get rid of an unwanted rental property, it's a great concept. I've covered this entire subject in *Real Estate Money Machine* (available at your local bookstores).

You'll see that you don't need a lot of money because you'll be using the same money over and over again. There are no banks, no tenants, no tying up money—no nothing—except creating positive cash flow.

I know a dentist in downtown Los Angeles who didn't want to be a dentist anymore. He attended my seminar and wanted to get going. He was going to take out a $50,000 loan on his house. I cautioned him not to. A $5,000 loan would be more than enough. He thought I was crazy. "If $5,000 is good, $50,000 has got to be better." I was insistent that the principle worked in those tough areas with very little money.

As a matter of fact, I think we make our best deals when we're poor, and we have to make the law of leverage our good friend. He got the $5,000 loan. I saw him seven months later, and he had already turned seven properties. His total net equity was $104,000 and generating $950 in net monthly income. He told me: "It was hard at first, but now I'm getting the hang of it. I guess I'll be able to quit dentistry in eight or nine more months now that I've got the system down. And you know what, Wade? I haven't even used $2,000 of the $5,000 I borrowed."

I have heard a thousand such stories since my book came out. I am gratified that it worked for me and doubly gratified as I see it working for others.

Summary

There are many ways to create cash flow. We've talked about five that are rather inclusive of all the ways. The one you choose depends not only on the games you want to play but also on how it will work for you in conjunction with the other methods. You may find yourself using all five methods on five different properties at the same time!

For centuries people have turned to real estate for rental income and the benefits gained when selling. However, it has only been in the past few decades that all the benefits of real estate have come together in such a cohesive package. The systems exist to create cash flow, and once they are created, they allow you to move on to many other areas. With this increase in income will come a different tax situation—now you're ready to invest to solve that problem. Those investments will spin off benefits and changes. The cycle is endless and challenging. Cash flow makes it all worthwhile.

CHAPTER 8

TAXES

Death and taxes may be inevitable, but death doesn't get worse every time Congress convenes. Since Congress and the IRS are the watchdogs of our money, we have to try to do everything in our power to keep our assets. Someone has estimated that for every dollar we invest, fifty-two cents ends up in some government agency. Let's buy more real estate and legally fight the system. You see, if we use real estate, two things happen: 1) we create an expense that allows us to keep more of our income for spending in this great country or for further investments and 2) we can become wealthy. We own the properties and they are growing in value and, we hope, in their ability to produce more income.

It's sad but true: when someone gets something without earning it, someone else has to earn something without getting it. When the government taxes production, we see less production. Why should someone do so much to make a profit (as in any business endeavor) and take all the risk? After all, if the quest is really successful, up to half of the profits goes to the government.

The one aspect of real estate that sets it apart from most other forms of investment is that the purchase can be written off. What is this write-off? It is the depreciation amount that the IRS lets us take and apply as an expense. Expenses are deductible, but it gets better when we're allowed to use this deduction to offset other income. You see, not only does the expense offset the profits (income) from the property creating the expense, but it can also offset income from other rental properties, or income from our "wages, salaries, and tips." It can also offset income in other years, as we will see later.

This depreciation expense is used extensively. In fact, more than half of the people investing in real estate are probably doing so just for the tax write-offs. As we know, many people work every day until noon for the government. Now, with real estate, that can be changed. Taxes won't go away. All we can do is fight legally by buying assets that let us keep our hard-earned money.

Take away the incentive to get rich and no one benefits. America allows us the right to be poor. That may sound funny, but think of what happens if everyone is forced to be mediocre. If we have the right to be poor, we also have the right to be rich.

I sat in amazement watching one political convention. A famous speaker came on and said the job of this party is to take the jar of jam off the top shelf and get it down to the bottom shelf so the little guy could eat it. The attendees stomped and hollered and clapped like crazy.

I sat in despair. If you take the jam away from the producer and then legislate away any incentive to replace it with a new jar, it will get eaten all right, and then nobody will have any. As someone once said, "Feed a man a fish and you've fed him for a meal. Teach a man to fish, and you've fed him for a lifetime."

I'm only bringing this up because this is the society we live in. And I don't think it's going to change too drastically. How can a government do anything rational more than one time in a row when it bans cigarette advertisements on TV and subsidizes tobacco farmers at the same time?

The increase in government spending and the IRS's "right" to take our money have led us to a serious dilemma. Let's put it in these terms. There is a game between us and the IRS in which up to 50% of our income is up for grabs on the game board. If we don't play the game, they can take all of our 50%. And worse yet, they have created all the rules of the game.

Tax his cow, Tax his goat

Tax his pants, Tax his coat

Tax his ties, Tax his shirt

Tax his work, Tax his dirt.

Tax his chew, Tax his smoke

Teach him taxes is no joke

Tax his car, Tax his gas

Tax the road he must pass

Tax his land, Tax his wage

Tax the bed in which he lays

Tax his tractor, Tax his mule

Tax the books used in school.

Tax him good and let him know

That after taxes he has no dough

If he hollers, Tax him more

Tax him till he's good and sore.

Tax his coffin, Tax his grave

Tax the sod in which he lays

Put these words upon his tomb

"Taxes drove me to my doom."

And when he's gone They don't relax

They'll still be after Inheritance Tax!

—Anonymous

Don't get me wrong. I'm as patriotic as the next guy, maybe more so. I love this country, but I believe that the government is here to serve the people and not the people to serve the government. I also believe the government that serves the American spirit the best is the government that does the least. Let it do only that which it has to do. Let people take care of themselves.

We can choose to go on and keep working for the IRS or fight back by building *financial security*, which does all kinds of good. President Reagan said true patriots do the latter. Let's keep our money working for us. Let's fix up neighborhoods, build and renovate houses, and rent and sell to people who don't qualify for bank loans. Let's hire carpenters, painters, CPAs, agents, and attorneys. Let's give muscle to the real estate industry by the activity we create. And if one of our motivations is to create tax shelters, then so be it. Let the chips fall where they may. There's too much good to be done in this life for ourselves and others to get into a personal war with the IRS.

I'm continually approached by people with seemingly great ways to get around IRS rulings. I'm amazed by how eloquent their arguments sound, but I can't see past their cheap polyester suits. The really wealthy people have just gotten better at the game than the IRS. Time can be invested or wasted. I know many millionaires who have become so by buying properties and investing to beat the IRS. Let's turn our disadvantages into advantages. The rulings will not go away. But I choose to live in this country, which means I have to play the game one way or the other. I choose to play it to win.

I sincerely hope these observations have shed some light on the subject so that you can make better decisions, because now I'll go through several ways real estate helps us be the expert. Whether you're a beginning or an experienced investor, rich or poor, I'm sure there are certain tax shelter aspects of real estate that will help you.

Down the Ladder

One of the most exciting by-products of real estate investing is this right to zero out on your taxes. How much in write-offs you'll need obviously depends on how much you're making. If you purchase a four-plex and it produces a break-even situation in the cash flow department, it will produce a big tax write-off. This depreciation expense travels through one or two tax forms and ends up on your 1040 form. There it does a world of good. It is a deduction to other income.

I calculate in a rough way that for every $10,000 of income you have, you'll need one good rental unit ($80,000 to $100,000 range). If you buy smaller properties, you'll need more units. You can figure it out in a few minutes on a calculator or in a few hours with your CPA.

Next Year—And Years To Come

It is important that we not only learn to zero out the current year so we can keep our current money, but also realize that our efforts affect other years as well. That's right. If we create losses this year that exceed this year's income, we may take those losses and apply them to the past two years.

We can actually go back two years and get back the taxes we paid, with interest, from the IRS. That's a check you'll relish. I teach this concept in depth in my seminars and wrote about it in my book, *Brilliant Deductions* (available at better bookstores). About half of the people attending my seminars have never heard of these NOL's (Net Operating Loss). Most wonder why their CPA's never told them about it, especially when they realize that real estate is the perfect vehicle to create such losses. It's perfect because you can buy the property with very little down (perhaps nothing) and may even be able to put cash in your pocket.

These losses are artificial. They are paper losses. Once they've been used to write off this year and go back two years, they then can be used in the future, for twenty years. The losses just sit and wait to pounce on any income as it comes up. You may even lose money (artificially) in many years to come and these NOL's may be accumulated year to year. They can run concurrently with each other. And you don't have to go back if it's not worth it. These losses might do more good if held for future use.

And now for the best thing about these NOL's. The properties you buy this year and hold will also produce tax write-offs next year. Oh, they probably won't be as high (the $9,000 will go to $8,000 or so), but they will be there nonetheless. I hope you understand the beauty of this. It means we can slow down and not work as hard.

Look at the amount of tax years that one year's efforts affect. It's 23: two back, 20 years into the future, and the current year. If that doesn't get your blood pumping, nothing will.

Just What Is It?

Now that we've seen what depreciation expense can do to create these write-offs and NOL's and the effect these NOL's have on other years, let's look at what they are.

In most other businesses, property and equipment are needed. If a lumber mill buys a new log saw for $100,000, it should have the right to write it off now. It's an expense right now. Not so, says the IRS. They say it is a capital investment and such items need to be capitalized or depreciated over their useful life. If their saw's useful life is five years, then the company may write it off at $20,000 per year.

In effect, this means that in five years the saw will be worthless. You can write it off your income and in theory will save money to replace it when it's obsolete, or whatever. Isn't this nice? They'll let the company write it off against the current income for five years even though it may have paid cash for it this year.

Luckily, most companies don't pay cash. They usually finance such purchases, but the IRS doesn't care. A purchase is a purchase no matter how you finance it. And this is the case with most real estate purchases. We purchase the $100,000 property with, say, $5,000 down. Now we pay off the balance at 11% at $950 per month.

Buildings may be written off in 27.5 years, and it may even be accelerated. The land may not be depreciated, but the appliances, carpets, and drapes may be written off in three and five years. That really gives a large deduction and allows us to buy less to produce more write-offs. The IRS form for figuring out this depreciation expense is even simple for once.

All this adds up to one big advantage for real estate. You may own property that makes $80,000 a year spendable income, but creates $120,000 in losses. The only problem you'll have is trying to convince your banker that you're really making money.

I strongly recommend that you surround yourself with a great team of specialists to help you out. I know that can be hard, and I really don't have any easy solutions to help you choose them. I went through six CPA's before I found a good one. I think that many CPAs just don't keep up.

Did you hear the joke about the two guys in a hot air balloon? They got lost and yelled to a man on the ground, "Where are we?"

The man replied, "You're in a hot air balloon."

One of the men looked at the other and said, "He's a CPA."

"How do you know?" asked the other.

"Because his information is totally correct and totally worthless."

Now, they're not all that bad. But consider yourself lucky if you find a good CPA. I've learned more from books and seminars than I ever did from my CPA or attorney. Then I go to them with this new-found information, and they say, "Yeah, that's a pretty neat deal, isn't it?" I wonder who should be paying whom sometimes.

At Risk

Let's go back to our $100,000 property. I think you now see the general idea behind the depreciation expense. One other thing needs mentioning, however. The purchase of this property is treated as if we paid cash for the entire thing. Think about that. Leverage is working at its best. We get all the benefits of ownership with just a fraction of the purchase price out of our pocket—the income, the growth, the write-offs.

Real estate is one of the few tax shelters left where it's possible to "lose" more than you have invested. Investments have an "at risk" rule. You may invest $10,000 in an offshore oil well, but if it loses, you may only write off the $10,000. We may buy our $100,000 property with $2,000 out of our pocket and write off the whole $100,000 (minus the land value) over 27.5 years. You really may only write off the purchasing price (plus improvements minus the land value) but you may write off an inordinately high amount in the first year.

Capital Gains

Let's discuss capital gains. After we use these great advantages and decide to sell the property, and if we owned it for at least eighteen months, it will only be taxed at the 20% bracket.

If our $100,000 property is now worth $120,000 and we sell for that, we'll only have to claim 40% of the $20,000 gain, or $8,000. I wrote "claim," not "pay." That $8,000 is claimed and applies to our tax situation. We can structure the sale to get the money when we need it—probably the first part of the year. You see, if we buy properties in January, we'll get $12/12$ths of the write off for that year. In February we'll get $11/12$ths, and so on to December, when we'll get $1/12$th. If you need write offs for any given year, it's best to buy properties as close to January as possible.

If a property you are selling is going to close in December, you may want to drag your feet and get it to close in January of the next year. Once again, wise planning is essential.

Wouldn't it be nice if we could do this to our income from our work or business and only pay 15 or 20% in taxes? Do you see why so many people invest in real estate? The taxes paid are half of what would be due from other businesses.

Recapture

We have been using these write-offs against current income at one hundred cents on the dollar. Investors are saving billions of dollars each year.

The depreciation expense that we take is subtracted each year from the original cost of a property. Our gain or profit is then determined by subtracting this new basis from the original price (plus improvements). Back to our $100,000 property. Let's say that over our few years of ownership we have written off $20,000. Any amounts taken by the straight-line method will be taxed at 25%. This is the property that just sold for $120,000. Our new gain is now $40,000. This is figured by taking the $120,000 minus the new basis of $80,000 ($100,000 original price minus $20,000 depreciation expense). $20,000 will be a long term capital gain taxed at 20%. $20,000 will be recaptured at 25%.

Can you believe it? All this time we've written it off and saved perhaps $6,000 to $12,000. That's money we can now keep. Even the $5,000 is like a tax-free, interest-free loan. We actually made $20,000 when the property sold. We don't even have to claim all of it when sold, and just look at the good the write-offs have done in the years we've owned the property. The law says that if you have been depreciating the property and then sell on an installment sales basis, you'll have to recapture in the year of sales the depreciation expense taken, just as if you sold for cash. A good tax professional can explain this to you.

One other thing. This property was purchased for $100,000 with $2,000 down, remember? The loan balance may only be paid down $1,000 more when we sell it. We still owe $97,000, but our cost basis is $80,000. The loan balance has nothing to do with the write-offs. The point I'm trying to make is that in all actuality, we've paid about $3,000 for $20,000 worth of write-offs. The rents could be going up and the property will be growing in equity. Incredible, isn't it?

Installment Sales
You will read a lot about installment sales in other chapters of this book, and I've covered the subject extensively in *Real Estate Money Machine* and in *Brilliant Deductions* (both available at your local bookstores), but it needs to be brought up here. Perhaps even with these great recapture rules, it might still be best for you to not sell this way and take your cash instead.

But instead of cash we may want to sell it and receive our money in several different tax years. You may receive any percentage as a down payment and then claim your profits as you receive them. Your profits will come in each month, but only a portion of the principal payment represents profit. You'll only have to claim that amount.

Back to our example for clarification. Suppose we sold the property for the $120,000, but instead we take a $10,000 down payment and our new buyer assumes our $97,000 loan balance. Our equity is now $13,000 ($120,000 minus the $10,000 down payment, minus the $97,000 loan assumed,) which we'll receive at $1,250 per month.   At the end of the year our principal received will be $600. The balance is interest.

We'll have to claim the interest and use the depreciation expense from other properties to shelter it. However, the gain is our main concern here. How much of each principal payment and the down payment is gain? We calculate this by using the installment sales ratio for the property.

Divide the gain by the selling price, or $120,000 divided by $20,000, or 16.6%. This means 16.6% of every principal payment will have to be claimed. Great! Now we can claim this percentage times the principal received over the next fifteen years or so. What a way to spread out our tax liability.

Trades
Today 1031 like-kind exchanges are very popular. You may want to dispose of a property by trading it into bigger and better units. You may do so and defer the gain time and time again. This is such a helpful way to use depreciated property. You see, after a while you may have very few tax write-offs left. If you sold, it could seriously affect your tax liability. In an exchange, you can exchange only your equity but then you may start depreciating the new, more expensive property.

There are a few other investments that allow this, but none with the support system (books, ideas, and gatherings) that real estate has. Call your stockbroker and say you want to exchange your corporate stock for a tax shelter. No way! You have to sell one (and pay taxes and commissions) and then buy the other one (with more commissions). Not so with real estate. You'll have hundreds of opportunities to trade your properties all over the country.

Interest

I won't belabor this here. We all know that interest paid on these loans is tax deductible. This just adds to the write-offs of each of our properties. Keep good track of it. It's a dollar-for-dollar expense.

Credits and Section 179 Property

Many parts of the purchase (or improvements) of real estate not only qualify for depreciation expenses but also actually become credits and attach directly to the amount due the IRS. These are not complicated, but because they are so potent, I really recommend that you go over the whole list with a good tax person.

While there, make sure you get all of the Section 179 property write-offs you can. We all have them. This used to be called "bonus first-year depreciation." It simply means that a specific dollar amount of depreciable items can be expensed right now and not depreciated. This amount may be just what you need to zero out. These items include computers, office equipment, tools, et cetera.

Are You Alone?

If you have the energy and talent, there are hundreds of people in your area with money. You can invest together, and you can divide up the benefits in different ways. Perhaps they can get the write-offs for putting up the money, and you can get the growth. This can support a negative cash flow and pick up part of the growth, and you share the tax write-offs. It's endless. This allows you to do more. You can get into and out of a lot of different properties this way.

Recapitulation

The following is an article that ran in *The Real Estate Connection*. I've updated it with the current tax laws. It recapitulates and molds together what I've stated so far and adds many other hints for wise tax planning:

> When it comes to taxes, most people are aware of the significant allowable deductions that they have coming. If you forget, the radio, TV, and print media will remind you of some of these things as tax preparers solicit your business. Medical deductions, interest payments, and regular property depreciation are all common items for deduction in order to reduce the amount of taxes due. This article will take the stand, however, that small details also all add up. Small details can add up to big deductions if you know what to look for. We have found that there are a number of tax deductions that most real estate investors overlook.
>
> **The Game Theory Of Taxes.** If you think about it, you'll come to realize that the IRS is playing a big game when it comes to taxes. The stakes are high too, namely, your money. Up to 50% of your income is on the line (depending on your tax bracket). You can't pull out of the game, either. Everyone has to play. So what should a person do?
>
> As long as you are required to play the game, you'd better learn the rules. Those who learn the rules and wisely use them to their advantage will be allowed to keep their income. The percentage of your income that you are allowed to keep is based on your knowledge and your skill. The better you are, the more you can keep, and if you learn the game well enough, you can even keep it all.
>
> The following are some of the commonly overlooked items that you, as a real estate investor, should be doing in order to offset your gains. We hope that you will find them enlightening and a source of tax savings in addition to those that you are already getting.
>
> **Day-To-Day Expen$e$.** Every business person has good intentions when it comes to record keeping, yet the most

commonly overlooked deductions are those everyday expenses that never get recorded. In some cases, it may not be a lack of record keeping as much as being unaware of the type of everyday deductions that are allowable.

Consider your auto expenses, for example. You, as a real estate investor, can deduct your auto expense when driving around looking for rental properties or houses that you wish to buy, fix up, and sell. Though often avoided because of the tedious nature of the task, keeping track of your mileage and maintenance will be very rewarding around April 15.

There are numerous other little day-to-day expenses that are often overlooked in the course of investing. How about little items such as Scotch tape or those FOR SALE and FOR RENT signs? Business lunches are something else you should be mindful of, as well as advertising expenses for each property and other promotional items such as business cards. You don't necessarily need to keep receipts for everything, either. Having receipts is good, but a notebook also works. Every time you have an expense, just write down the date, the amount, the place, what it was for, and who you were with. Good records are sufficient for IRS purposes.

Another day-to-day expense that is often overlooked is a gift. You may deduct up to $25 per gift, and the recipient doesn't even have to claim it! Gifts to employees are among those that are allowed.

Carry backs/Carry overs. As an investor, you probably find that your income fluctuates from year to year. Some years you will make large amounts of money from the sale of some of your holdings. Other years you may make smaller amounts because you are hanging onto your properties.

If you've heard me speak, you understand how to handle such a situation. One way in particular is by creating NOL's (Net Operating Losses), which stem mainly from depreciation allowances or, in other words, an artificial paper loss. Once you have created these NOL's, you must decide how to handle them. Your option is either to have them apply to the current year and the past two, then up to twenty years in the future, or to skip the past years and have them apply strictly to the future years. The determining factor is your income. Did you make a lot of money in one or two of the past years and, consequently, pay a lot of taxes at that time? If so, then you might want to use the carryback technique to recover that amount (with interest) from the IRS. Perhaps you didn't make that much money in the past, but are going to make large amounts of money in the future. In this case, you might opt to not go back with your NOL, but just go forward.

Remember also, you can have more than one NOL going at a time (see *Brilliant Deductions* for more details on this point).

Travel For Investments. No matter where you currently live, there are probably other parts of the country that you enjoy visiting. Winter is a great time for people in the northern states to head for warmer climates. It's also a great time for the fair-weather residents to head for the famous ski slopes for a week or two of fun. Many people are taking these trips and writing off portions of them as an expense. This is accomplished by buying some sort of investment property in the area you enjoy visiting. Two, perhaps three times a year, you will go to that area to check on your investment, evict a tenant, hire work done, or whatever. While you are there, you are able to enjoy yourself with a little skiing or beachcombing, whichever the case might be. All the expenses associated with "business" (including the travel there and back) are fully deductible. The portion of expense that was for private use is not. Although absentee management isn't always a good idea, it can sometimes work to an investor's advantage (and pleasure).

Accelerated Depreciation. The depreciation-expense deduction allows an investor to recover the costs of income-producing property. This expense produces deductions that do not cost anything. You might say, then, that this deduction is artificial in nature. You may claim this deduction either in a straight-line or an accelerated method.

Taxes

Most people are familiar with the straight-line method, so we won't take time to explain it here. Many people, however, are not familiar with the MACRS (Modified Accelerated Cost Recovery System) method, which allows a standard useful life for equipment, and furnishings of 27.5 years. What this means for you is that you can write the furnace, office, and so on in 27.5 years. Once you pencil this method out in comparison to straight-line depreciation, you will see the obvious advantages.

Straight-line is a method of taking the depreciating expense in equal amounts over the years chosen. MACRS on the other hand is accelerated in the first few years and then declines to an amount even less than the straight-line method in the remaining years.

One important thing to keep in mind, however, is that if you decide to use this method (MACRS), the values of the different types of property must be established at the time you purchase the property.

Bonus First Year Depreciation/Section 179. Although the new tax laws have made this aspect less of an advantage than it used to be for real estate investors, there still are some real advantages under the new Section 179 that you should be aware of.

In an effort to increase investments by the small-business investors, the first-year bonus-depreciation has been changed. Previously, this included the right to deduct 20% of the cost of qualifying property and to write it off in the year of acquisition. This format, however, has been repealed. Now, a new Section 179 expense deduction has taken its place. It is provided for taxpayers who elect to treat the cost of qualifying property (Section 179 property) as an expense rather than as a capital expenditure. This change took effect in 1982.

The election to treat property in this fashion must: 1) specify the item to which it applies, 2) specify the portion of the cost of each item to be deducted currently, and 3) be made on an original return (including extensions).

There is an annual dollar limitation on the aggregate cost that may be expensed in any given year. The following table shows those limits as they now are and as they will be in the future:

If the taxable year begins in:	The applicable amount is:
1997	$18,000
1998	$18,500
1999	$19,000
2000	$20,000
2001 or 2002	$24,000
2003 or thereafter	$25,000

The balance of the cost needs to be capitalized and depreciated over its MACRS life.

The only hitch to this whole deduction is that property held for the production of income does not qualify. How then can an investor take advantage of Section 179? If property that is not considered the main structure is purchased (stoves, refrigerators, separate air-conditioning units) for business use, it will fall under this category and will qualify for this effective way of writing it off.

Tax Credit. To better understand this deduction, let us first point out an important issue. A tax credit is not to be confused with a tax deduction. There is a big difference. A tax deduction comes off your adjusted income, but a tax credit is applied directly to your tax liability.

Abusive Tax Shelters

The next few years will see many headlines about tax shelters. I strongly believe that these shelters are good for the country. They keep money circulating. They keep money in the hands of the people where it should be, and they give hope to our otherwise dismal April 15. For example, I own a percentage of some hotels. My statements include amounts that are spent on remodeling, but that money is now in the hands of masons, gardeners, carpenters, and roofers. Furthermore, do you wonder what the previous owners are doing with the money they received? They are probably buying more, fixing them up, and trying to live the American Dream the best way they can.

I'll now include a few ways to avoid abusive shelters so you won't send up any red flags.

The IRS examines many things when deciding whether or not to investigate a tax shelter for its legitimacy. The points covered by the IRS can also prove helpful to investors when considering possible investment in a tax shelter. The following points are ones investors would do well to consider before committing their money:

Low Rate of Return: the IRS will take notice of a shelter in which the present value of all future income is less than the present value of all the investment and associated costs of the shelter. This would indicate that the primary goal of the investment is tax avoidance.

Other items that catch the eye of the IRS include:

- Cash return compared to risk.

- Is the lease a lease or a sale?

- The transfer of the burden and benefits of ownership.

- Is the transaction a sale or an option, lease or security device?

- The relationship of price to fair market value.

- Any buildup of equity.

Inflated Sales Price: an inflated sales price is used to inflate the basis, causing higher depreciation deductions. The investment should be consistent with fair market value in order to escape the scrutiny of the IRS.

Front End Load: often syndications try to deduct large payments in the first year that are paid to the general partner and/or to "outsiders." This is not meant to imply that all front end fees are illegitimate. They are, however, subject to very strict scrutiny by the IRS.

For example, some expenses are deductible only over a period of at least five years. These might include expenditures that are incident to the creation of the partnership, and chargeable to the capital account and have an ascertainable life. The cost of promoting the sale of a partnership interest would be considered an organizational expense. Legal fees, accounting incident to organizing the partnership, and filing fees are all considered organizational expenses.

Fees not considered to be organizational expenses that require capitalizing include:

- Expenses incurred for the removing or admitting of partners after the original organizations

- Registration fees

- Legal fees of underwriter for securities and tax advice

- Brokerage fees for syndication

- Expenses for acquiring assets

The IRS also takes a very close look at transactions that involve certain financing schemes. These include:

Nonrecourse Financing: one big red flag for the IRS here is when a loan is way out of line with the fair market value of the property. If the loan amount is much greater than the value of the property, the loan may be treated as contingent, and thus completely excluded from the basis.

Wraparound Mortgages: most wraps are legitimate. However, sometimes they are used to inflate the purchase price above fair market value. At other times, they may be used to generate large prepaid interest deductions—that is, instead of just giving a note to the seller and taking the property subject to the existing mortgage, the investors make a large deductible payment.

There are many other areas we could cover, but for now, let me just say that your investments should clearly be for the purpose of making a profit and not just for creating tax write-offs. This simple rule will, for the most part, keep you out of trouble.

On September 1, 1984, the IRS initiated the requirement that most tax shelters be registered with the federal government. Each shelter will be assigned a registration number, which investors will have to include on their federal income tax returns. According to former IRS commissioner Margaret Milner Richardson, the purpose of the registration requirement is to help gather information about the number, kind, and size of tax shelters being offered.

Summary

I'll end this chapter with a quotation from Thomas Edison, who said it better than I could:

> There is far more danger in public monopoly than there is in private monopoly, for when the government goes into business, it can always shift its losses to the taxpayers. If it goes into the power business, it can always pretend to sell cheap power, and then cover up its losses. The government never really goes into business, for it never makes ends meet, and that is the first requisite of successful business. It just mixes a little business and politics, and no one ever gets a chance to find out what is actually going on.

CHAPTER 9

EQUITY GROWTH

Of the three biggest reasons for real estate investing, equity growth takes the third seat, but only because income and tax relief reasons need immediate attention. This is probably the way it should be. After all, how can we plan for the future when our after-tax income is so small now?

As investors we devote an inordinate amount of time creating more income and tax write-offs. Because we're busy doing this, a by-product occurs. The properties that we're buying increase in value. In a short while we have equities. Then we start looking for several things to do with them. I'll spend a lot of time in this chapter exploring the fascinating things that can be done, but before I do, let's get into equity creation.

Defining Equity

There are many measuring systems, but let's keep it simple: equity is what you own. If your property is a rental unit, your equity will be the difference between the fair market value of the property and your outstanding loans. It has nothing to do with purchase or selling price.

If, for example, you purchased a duplex for $60,000 with $3,000 down and took over loans of $50,000—giving the seller a note for his remaining balance of $7,000—and then put $2,000 into fixing it up, raising the value (because of market comparables and the formula attached to rents) to $70,000, your equity will be $13,000.

$60,000   Purchase price

($3,000)   Down payment

$57,000   Current loans payable

$70,000   New appraised value

$13,000   Equity — ($70,000 - $57,000 = $13,000)

The down payment and fix-up costs help create the equity and will determine yields, and so on, but that's the extent of it as far as equity is concerned.

If you now sold the property by letting someone give you $5,000 down on the $70,000 price and take over your $57,000 loans, your equity will be $8,000 in the form of a note receivable. Yes, your cash is equity, but it is no longer associated with this property. It's freed up and available to go to work again.

If you sold the property on a wraparound contract or mortgage, or an all-inclusive trust deed with the same $5,000 down, you will create a $65,000 note receivable to you and you will maintain the $57,000 loan, keeping the loan and payments in your name.

This is the Money Machine concept. You have your invested cash back in the form of the $5,000 down payment, and it's ready to go to work again. The only difference is that now equity is determined by the difference between what someone owes you and what you owe someone else. In this case it will be:

$65,000   Receivable note

($57,000)   Payable loan

$ 8,000   Equity

Before we move on, let's point out a few other differences. You are now collecting and making payments, which may be a little time-consuming but well worth it when you consider that you're still in control of the bottom loans. You can make sure that they get paid. If anything goes wrong, you're there to take care of it. Many people try to shun this responsibility and clear out, but I recommend staying in control and being the middleman, all payments come and go through you.

One other thing that makes this plan so great is that the older loans that you've assumed and the new one that you've created for the seller probably have lower interest rates than the new wraparound loan to your buyer. What this really means is that these loans have more of the monthly payment going to principal. For example, let's say we have a $600 payment on our $57,000 in loans, and $70 of that amount is principal—the remainder, of course, being interest and perhaps taxes and insurance. Now, let's say that our buyer is paying us $700 on the $65,000 note receivable, of which only $40 is principal. What we have is a $30 per month equity growth.

Our payables usually pay off faster than our receivables. This also looks great on our financial statement in that our net is growing by $30 a month and all we're doing is collecting and making payments.

"What about the future appreciation of the property," you ask? That obviously goes to your new buyer; but remember, you have the $5,000 down payment, so you can go do it again (and again).

The faster principal paydown on the bottom loans brings up another interesting item. The loans pay off in less time. Back to our example. Let's say the $57,000 is actually three different loans. One is $23,000 at 10%, which will pay off in 17 years; another is $27,000 at 10%, which will pay off in 19; and another is a $7,000 loan we created to the seller, which will pay off in 10 years at 10.25%.

Our loan receivable, however, is at 11% and will pay off in twenty-six years. You can see what will happen when the older loans start to drop off—we'll get to keep more of the monthly payment coming in to us. Isn't this exciting? Just think what will happen if we take the down payment that we received and repeat this, time and time again.

There are other types of equities (cash flow and tax write-offs), but they are all associated with one of the three just mentioned. A limited partnership owns properties, and equity is created there. Equities are nice if they are created properly and nicer still if they give off an income stream.

Creating Equity

For many years seminar companies all over the country have told attendees to buy, buy, buy, and then just sit back and wait for the properties to grow in value. This worked for many people. Investing in real estate was easy. Everyone had the Midas touch. It was even possible to buy wrong and then wait until the appreciation corrected the problem. Real estate was very forgiving. It still is, but everyone should be more cautious now.

I suggest that we all abandon the concept that all we have to do is buy and wait. Even if the growth is there, we have no control over inflation in general. Even when I first started, I thought that what American inflation did to the value of properties was just icing on the cake. I'm not saying that I haven't taken advantage of it—only that I wanted no part of my investment plan to rely on something I couldn't control.

Paintbrush Inflation

The only type of inflation I like is one that I can control. Let me give an example of what type of property I look for and you'll see my concept clearly.

- I look for a property way under market value.

- I hope it will just be messy—needing only a few repairs.

- I hope the property has value-potential. This means that the neighborhood must be nice and that the property can be purchased substantially below the other houses in the neighborhood.

- The down payment has to be right—maintaining enough cash to do the fixing up. I hope that I can pay the down payment later, when I sell or refinance it.

- All of the purchase terms have to be conducive to my selling the property. I'll walk away from due-on-sale clauses, and so on, that may cause problems in the future.

- It has to be in the area of movement—no diminishing communities. I look for people coming and going. I need to get back all of my money. This probably means I can't put in very much. I want all of my doors to be open when I sell.

Once I've found such a property, I'm assured that I'm not trading cash for someone else's equity. I don't consider that a fair trade. A small amount of cash for a lot of potential is what I'm looking for.

Once purchased, it's just a matter of arranging the cleaning and fix-up. At first, when money is tight, you may have to do some of that yourself, but I strongly recommend that you find others who may be more qualified to do it. Remember, your time is best spent elsewhere. You are valuable as an investor—much less so as a carpet layer, but I realize that there are many people out there who want to fix up houses.

Foreclosures

The best and most technical way to find super bargains is to get involved in the foreclosure process. My book *How To Pick Up Foreclosures* covers this area of investment in detail, but there is a point to be made here. For real estate investors, foreclosures represent a gold mine. At the same time, it also takes some understanding of the personal side of the situation in order to deal with the emotions involved. I hope this will give you, the investor, some insight into the personal side of the homeowner who faces losing his home.

The first step to understanding the people you will be dealing with when trying to pick up foreclosures in their early stages is to try to see the problem from their point of view. They probably already know that they are behind in their house payments, and they are being hassled by the bank or whomever it is that holds the mortgage. Most of these people feel that they will be able to solve their own problems, and most of them will. It is becoming more common, however, especially with credit and tight money policies, that individuals who feel they have an ace up their sleeve by going to the bank are now finding themselves out of luck. They are not able to borrow the money, and chances are, neither are their friends or relatives. Their sources, for the most part, have all dried up. Somehow, though, people think they can just walk into a bank, explain their situation, and have the bank understand their circumstances and be willing to work with them. In most cases, however, the bank will see it as a matter of dollars and cents. Their concern will be for their interest only.

One major reaction of people whose houses are in jeopardy is disbelief. They can't believe that anything like this is happening to them. You may even take the legal notice right up to them, show them their name and address, and not have them believe you. By the time they realize what the state of their situation really is, it is often too late. Their house is beyond saving, and it is being auctioned right out from under them.

Often the investors who pursue foreclosures are pinned with a bum rap. They are labeled opportunists who are taking advantage of people at a very trying time in their lives. This may be true with some investors. They may, indeed, walk away with everything, with no consideration for the people with whom they are dealing. We would like to think that such instances constitute the minority of cases. Unfortunately, it only takes the bad acts of a few to tarnish the reputation of many.

The truth of the matter is that, in reality, if you take over the house, you are doing homeowners a big favor. Consider, for a moment, the consequences involved if a foreclosure goes all the way through the process and the homeowners lose their homes against their wishes.

Obviously, the first reaction to such a happening is the deterioration of their credit rating. Minor problems like being late on monthly payments will stay on a credit report for about three years. A major foreclosure, like the one we are talking about here, will stay on the homeowners' credit reports for up to seven years. They may, therefore, be unable to purchase another house for the duration of that seven-year period. In most cases, they will have a hard time purchasing anything at all on credit.

Self-esteem also falls prey to the foreclosure action. It's hard for people to face themselves, their families, and their friends once everyone knows that their house was taken from them for nonpayment. Without self-esteem to keep a person going, a speedy recovery from such a situation is highly unlikely. One failure such as this can lead to another, then another.

If real estate investors enter the picture before the house hits the auction or before the cure date, they are in a position to save the homeowners' credit rating and self-esteem. If the investors and the homeowners come to an agreement and the homeowners quitclaim the property to the investors, the monkey is at that point taken off the homeowners' backs. The investors have assumed the liabilities (which is one reason to check out the exact liabilities before signing on the dotted line) and therefore will be making the back payments. The homeowners are then freed from the situation and their credit is saved.

As far as saving the homeowners' self-esteem, the investor can help there also. First, by relieving the homeowners of the liability, the investor is also saving them the possible shame that could arise from the situation. Also, as a gesture of thanks, the investor could offer an amount of money to the homeowners to help them on their way and perhaps give them the small boost they need to face tomorrow and the many tomorrows to follow.

This was intended to help you and encourage you to try to understand the individuals you will be dealing with while trying to pick up foreclosures. At the same time, be cautious not to let their problems become your problems. You may face a situation where the homeowners, after telling you their sad tales, will ask you to loan them the money and save them from the fate that lies ahead. Somewhere at this point, you should draw the line. Understand that what you are offering them in your initial offer is already of great benefit to them. Investing is your business, and you must keep those aspects of the transaction in mind and in line.

Just think how effective you'll be if you become an expert at finding super deals. If you can have a list of potential buyers and other investors, it will make your job much easier.

Making It Fast

Most of us don't have years to wait to "make it." If we have to buy just one property and wait for it to appreciate, it may be a long wait. That's why it's so exciting that new concepts—like the Money Machine concept—have been developed and work so well.

You don't have to wait. If you buy right, you can quickly create equity. To summarize the two ways to build up equity quickly, I only need to mention (1) good deals and (2) cosmetic paintbrush inflation, and your creative mind and hard work can take over and get going.

Equity Growth

Most people understand that equity growth is important and that it can and should depend on you. The answer is tied up in all the things you can do with it. Can we treat it like money? How hard (or easy) is it to work with? How will it affect my future?

What do we want it to do? That's the key question, and the answers are many and exciting. Real estate is very versatile in this area. I'll point out several ideas here in an effort to get your creative juices flowing. You'll quickly realize that no other form of investment gives you even a fraction of these advantages. Is it any wonder why so many people who looked to stocks and gold for growth are now investing in real estate and why very few real estate investors have changed to stocks?

More Income And Benefits Later

Why are we all working so hard anyway? Isn't it so we can retire later or at least slow down and enjoy life a little more? It doesn't matter what technique is used to create the growth, just as long as it means more income in the future.

With a house, either the rents will increase or the monthly income from notes will be created (increased probably, if on a wrap). The equity can be sold for cash or traded into other properties. Remember, you're in control of this growth. Good solid equities mean a lot to others, so they should mean a lot to you.

Borrowing against equities has gained in popularity. Why? Because you don't have to pay taxes on borrowed money. Just think about finding a great house—say $10,000 under market. A few thousand dollars of fix-up and you've increased that to $15,000 to $20,000. Now, you go to a bank for a loan and get back your down payment and fix-up costs, which are then ready to go to work again, and you have the rest of the loan money for whatever—tax free. And the interest paid to the bank is tax deductible.

Summary

Increased income, selling or trading, and borrowing power are advantages of real estate investing that never go away. If we plant the seeds, we'll reap the harvest. It's nice to know that we can have so much potential in our future.

On the following page is a copy of the actual flyer I used. This "I Buy Houses" flyer, is specially designed and people-tested. Sellers will be contacting you after receiving it to see if you will buy their homes.

I BUY HOUSES!

I AM NOT A REAL ESTATE AGENT
I AM NOT ASSOCIATED WITH ANY
REAL ESTATE FIRM.

Do you need to sell your house? You may be transferred, or need a bigger or smaller house. You may be having financial difficulties and risk losing your house. Maybe you've experienced a divorce or death that forces you to move. Whatever the case, I'd be more than happy to talk with you about buying your house.

I want to buy houses that I can fixup to resell. Or houses that would make good rentals. I am specifically looking for houses that need painting, landscaping, new roofs and other improvements. No job is too large or small. If you have a problem finding someone to buy your house, look no further!

Just give me a call.
Save Closing Costs

Call:

YOUR
Name
Address
and Phone

By the way, I may have some houses for sale, also. Give me a call and I'll try to get you into a house of your own!

CHAPTER 10

THE REAL ESTATE MONEY MACHINE

These past few years have been very enlightening. I've had the opportunity to be on several hundred radio and TV talk shows. At almost every one, the host has commented on my first book's title: *Real Estate Money Machine*. The most frequent remark is that it sounds like a get-rich-quick formula. My usual comeback is that it is just the opposite. I tell the host that when I was writing the book, the publisher said, "Look, Wade, we've got a hundred books on how to make a million dollars, can you write a book on how to make a living?"

It took a long time to come up with that title. And even though only a few people have said it correctly when introducing me, every word does have its place. Money doesn't grow on trees, and it doesn't come from a machine. The concept, though, is to build an investment portfolio that continually gives off monthly income with very little start-up capital.

It's fun to share this concept here in brief form. The book has done very well, and letters come in from everywhere, proving that a single concept repeated often enough will bring success. And once you've seen this concept, you'll realize two things: 1) it is true what the president of Wham-O said, "I'd rather lose money and know how I lost it than make money and not know how I made it." If we can do something repetitiously, we can become good at it, refine it, analyze it, and retire on it. It's not that the job becomes easier, it's that our ability to do it becomes better and (2) this is no get-rich-quick scheme. It takes many long hours of learning and doing. There are many a "no" on our way to the "yes," but it is attainable, and it sure beats the alternatives.

That last sentence is a good diving board to get us into the pool. For a long time there were two philosophies for investing in real estate. One philosophy was to buy a property, fix it up, then find someone to get a new loan and pay you off. You would then take the money and do it again, only this time with a larger property. You kept repeating this process. It still works today on certain properties if they are purchased right, but the banks are in too much control, and it's almost impossible to stay on track because the investor is out of control with most of the process.

The other philosophy is to buy and hold onto the property one day short of forever. There are a lot of seminars teaching this method. This plan is also good if you buy low and get low payments, but it has two major drawbacks: the first drawback is that it usually takes a small amount of cash for the down payment and closing costs, and most people can afford only one property. Then they have to save up or borrow to get a second down payment. The second drawback is that they become a landlord and have all the attendant problems. I've been there. It's hard to get started and find that all you ever do is make repairs. In today's marketplace there's so little profit (with the higher than usual monthly payments and rents that haven't kept up) that it seems as if landlords end up working for minimum wage.

The last thing I'll write about these two philosophies is that they just take too darn long. Most people get frustrated and just give up. While the Money Machine concept is not a get-rich-quick scheme, it sure isn't a get-rich-slow plan either. It is a sensible proven way to make good money—real money because it solves the need for a steady monthly income. Hard work is needed to build it, but then the money just keeps rolling in.

I'll spend the next several pages explaining the process and telling you what a few others are doing, but first it would be helpful to explain the concept in a few sentences. Test me as you read the pages after the next paragraph and see if I deviate. Everything is part of a puzzle. We can't go on to C until we've done B. Remember, repetition is the byword.

The Money Machine concept is a system of buying properties 1) under market value and 2) with assumable loans, and hopefully where the sellers will take their equity (or most of it) on monthly payments. Then, the property is fixed up cosmetically and resold with the investors getting back the money they have put in and taking monthly payments for their newly created equity. The investors have created a lien on the property, and that is their security.

If that sounds like a mouthful, it is. But, like any concept, once it is explained and understood, you will say, "Aha!" It's like learning the secret to a magic trick.

Buying

We have to buy right. The word "right" means that the terms and conditions of buying have to be conducive to selling. People often ask: "What if I can't sell it?" I truthfully reply: "Don't buy it." Only buy what you can resell. A good house in a fair to good neighborhood is the right choice. Buy in lower-middle-income neighborhoods. If you see people jogging, leave. Those are the wrong neighborhoods. Blue collar workers don't come home and go jogging. Blue collar areas are the right neighborhoods to invest in because it's where most people live. One other point: people getting rich and people getting poor have to live in the neighborhoods. We'll get them coming and going.

Buy houses with assumable loans. You're not going to hide anything from the banks, so if it is going to be a problem, don't buy that house. Look for homes with low to moderate interest rates. The older FHA and VA loans are fully assumable. It costs only a small name change fee. There is no qualifying by you or anyone who may own the property in the future.

We're obviously looking for diamonds in the rough. The old adage about buying the worst house in the best neighborhood is still the best advice.

Constantly be looking or have others looking for you. Carry a promissory note and a purchase agreement in the glove compartment because good deals are everywhere. Also keep in mind that, at first, finding these good deals seems like the hardest thing to do, but after a few weeks or a few months, when you've been on the streets, this will be the easiest part.

The hard part is to find people who are willing to take monthly payments for their equity. Most people want cash. We need to get to the people before they've mentally spent their money so we can educate them on the beauty of monthly payments. I love monthly payments and would rather have $100 a month for twenty-two years than $10,000 cash, especially when I create the $100 from virtually nothing. If you think you'll have a hard time explaining to people why they should take monthly payments from you instead of a lump sum, you can show them a pamphlet I've written that explains all the reasons why monthly payments are beneficial. It's called *"Owner Financing,"* and because it's only 53 pages, it will be convenient for prospective sellers to read. If you want a copy, just send $5.95 to the publisher, Lighthouse Publishing Group, Inc. at 14675 Interurban Avenue South, Seattle, Washington, 98168-4664, or call 1-800-872-7411.

Back to the process. The main thing to remember when buying is to guard your cash. When you sell, it has to be a good deal for the next person, and if you're demanding too much down, you won't find a buyer. When I buy, my average down payment is 4% of the purchase price, and when I sell, the average down payment I receive is 6% of the new selling price.

While "down payments in" and "down payments out" are important, the whole process bogs down if the monthly payments are out of line. When average people buy a property, they have to think about many things: the purchase price, the down payment, the monthly payments, the interest rate, and so on. Of these concerns, the monthly payment required either makes or breaks the deal. If this aspect is so important to the next person who will buy the house (or rent it for that matter), should it not be our number one consideration when we are buying? This is called "second generation thinking." Most of us get bogged down thinking first generation. We just think of ourselves: how we like the house, how the monthly payment affects us, how we respond to the neighborhood, and so on. Most problems in real estate investing wouldn't occur if the investor would think about the next person: the second generation.

Handle the purchase by the book. Use competent professionals to take care of details such as drawing up the papers, obtaining an escrow company, title insurance, and others. Then, sell right.

Fix-Up

This will not be a lengthy section as I have a whole chapter on fixing up in *Real Estate Money Machine.* The main idea, once again, is to guard our cash. If some people want to fix up a house fit for a king, let them. Instead, let's just do light cosmetic work and general cleanup. The fix-up we do should be to enhance and sell the already good deal that we've purchased.

Here are five recommendations that will prove the point. Others will occur to you when you get in the middle of a project and ask yourself the question: "What else could I be doing with my time and money?"

1. Fix up your houses for women. Women buy real estate. The final decision is theirs. I'm reminded of a story about a man up in Heaven. There were two doors. One door was marked "For Henpecked Husbands," and there was a long line of men standing in front of it. The other door was marked "For Men Who Are the Boss," and there was only one man standing in front of that door. When asked why he was standing there, he replied, "I don't know, my wife told me to." Women control the purchase of real estate.

2. Use one color of paint in all your houses and apartments. A nice off-white is best. It goes with everything and makes small rooms look larger. Using one color

will also save you a lot of money because you can buy
it in larger quantities; also you don't have numerous
paint cans lying around with all different colors of
paint left over in your garage.

3. Don't dicker with your subcontractors on the price of
    fixing up. If you compromise on the amount of money
    you'll pay them, the quality of their work will go
    down.

4. Commit people working on your houses to an ending
    time for their work. If you don't, the job won't get done
    on time—and guess who gets stuck with making
    payments on a vacant house?

5. Buy wholesale. You don't need a license. Just tell
    hardware, plumbing, and electrical stores that you're
    remodeling many houses and want to set up an ac-
    count. At one time we made contact with a carpet firm
    in Chattanooga near the carpet manufacturing capital
    of the world in Georgia, named Complete Carpet
    Service, to buy carpet direct for $2 to $4 a yard, and
    some really good FHA carpet for $6 or so per yard.
    They shipped it right to the house or building we were
    fixing up. There are many companies that will do
    business with you this way. To join their clubs and
    receive a portable sample board with three grades and
    different prices for you to see the color and quality,
    you can send $20 to them. Tell them you read my book
    and want the Carpet Sample Board. The money will be
    deducted from your first order. This alone should save
    you several hundred dollars per property.

In short, guard your cash. If you put too much in, you're back
to the waiting game to get it out. As I've wanted this chapter to
dwell on the Money Machine concept in general and not get too
far into the specifics, please see Chapter 14 (Other Investment
Tips) for many more hints on evaluating and doing repair work.

Selling

So far there has been a method to our madness. Everything has to make sense, and now that the property is livable, let's sell it. The terms of selling definitely have to be a good deal for the next person. Many people are renting today because they can't afford the monthly payments. If people can rent a $60,000 house for $500 a month, why should they purchase it for $700 plus per month?

Every detail has to be fair. The down payment we charge has to be under 10% of the new selling price. We can charge more, but we'll probably have to wait. The interest rate should be low, if possible, so the payment can stay affordable. The price should also be slightly under market value so some profit is left for the next person. We buy low and sell just below high.

In every other business, profits are made when something is sold. Granted, there are many advantages to holding real estate, but the selling aspect is so often overlooked. I contend that the way to faster profits is to treat the investments like a business. Nothing works unless the selling of the property is a good deal for the next person.

This concept is not complicated. Your horse sense will get you over the hurdles. Map out a plan and minimize the obstacles. Why go to all this trouble? Because when it's time to sell, we want to have all of our doors open. We want to be able to sell the property in any way we please. If we've taken on a loan with a due-on-sale clause, many doors slam closed. If we put in too much money, the door of selling with very little down on a wraparound or assumption closes. Keeping all of our doors open takes cautious planning.

And remember, since at some point you'll want to sell, make sure all the terms and conditions of buying are conducive to selling. It doesn't take much to figure out that being cautious in buying the property and taking care to safeguard all future possibilities force us to make a good deal. Another case for doing things right is that doing them right works for us behind our back.

Just think of the alternatives—if we don't do this kind of planning and structuring, the results can be horrendous. Most of the problems I have gotten into, or now hear about, have their origin in the financing arrangements of purchasing the property. If this is the case, then let's be careful. All of our efforts for good leverage and tax write-offs can go out the window with just one clause that restricts our right to sell. Be prepared to walk away from a bad deal rather than get the deal and not be able to sleep at night.

We don't want to create new problems by selling; selling should be done to solve problems, not create them. So our first step in selling is to see how it will affect our other investments, especially our tax situation. It's amazing how fast the selling of one property affects the amount of taxes we would have to claim if we sold another one. We can go marching up through the tax brackets pretty quickly.

Real estate is so great because we are not limited to just one way of selling. It's fun because we can use different methods to solve different problems. We could hit a single (installment sale for the entire amount) and advance a little with very few tax implications, but with great monthly income. We could hit a double by getting some money down and carrying the balance. We could even hit a homer and get all of our money.

Perhaps we should wait for a while. The property might be a good rental unit, but the time to hit isn't right. We could even send in our designated hitter: switch the property for something else on a tax-deferred exchange. And it could be that after a few successful deals, we could take our mitt and ball and play a different game. I'm not recommending this—I'm just bringing up a possibility.

It's important and comforting to know that these selling methods are available. I suppose so many different ways have been developed with so many different tax savings because so many people own and use real estate for their income, growth, and tax purposes. So let's explore some of the aspects of these ideas.

Cashing Out

Sometimes this way is the preferred method, especially if there is a lot of money tied up or there are huge equities. For further ideas on huge equities and how to deal with them see my book, *Real Estate Money Machine*. We can accomplish this by having our buyer get new bank financing. We can help out by quickly getting the information the bank needs, or we could possibly lend the buyer the down payment by taking back a second or third mortgage.

Cashing out has an effect on your tax bracket, so you should watch this. Make sure other strategies (holding properties as rentals) are in place. If not, you may have to pay some taxes, but remember, it is possible to get this year's taxes back for three years in the future (see Chapter 8 "Taxes" in this book).

These questions always come up: what else could you be doing with the money? Are you willing to play the game with the IRS or the banks to get the property sold? Will you benefit more with the excess cash? Do you have other properties that you can get into? Are they lined up and ready to go?

Cashing out is one of the greatest enhancers to any investment plan. From all of my experience, though, I have found that he who relies solely on cashing out hoes a long row. It's nice, but there are other alternatives. What I'm suggesting here is this: don't go chasing after cash, but if cash comes chasing after you, take it.

Installment Sales

This section is not designed to give all of the particulars of an installment sale but only to give the highlights. I've covered the subject extensively in my other books. An installment sale is one in which you receive payments in two or more tax years.

There are three advantages to such a sale:

Tax Savings: when you make a gain on a property you have to claim it, but with an installment sale, you can claim the gain as you receive it. This means that if you are receiving payments for 28 years, then each year you'll claim the gain and pay taxes on it in that same year.

How much you will pay is determined by figuring out the installment sales ratio for each property sold. Note: if the property qualifies for long-term capital gains treatment, then you'll only have to claim that amount. For example, if you bought a four-plex for $80,000 and sold it for $100,000 a year later (currently, property held for longer than six months qualifies for such treatment) you would only have to claim 40% of the gain (current rate). In this case it would be 40% of the $20,000 gain, or $8,000 ($100,000 minus $80,000 = $20,000 x 40% = $8,000). This amount would transfer to your 1040 form through your Schedule D and affect your tax situation in some way. If the property were held short and then sold on contract, mortgage, All Inclusive Trust Deed (AITD), or any type of owner-financing, you would determine what you need to pay by figuring out the installment sales ratio. You do this by simply dividing the profit (or gain) by the selling price (in this case it would be $20,000 divided by $100,000 = .2, or 20%). This means 20% of the principal payments represents gain. The other 80% represents return of the cost basis (remember the $80,000).

In this example it comes out evenly at 20%. Usually it will be several decimal places over because very few deals are just zeros. With the current tax law, you'll have to recapture any depreciation expense in the year of sale.

Now that the ratio is determined (and we use IRS Form 6252 to calculate all of this), we take that ratio times the amount of principal payments ($50 per month x 12), and we add the down payment ($5,000). The total received is $5,600. We now claim 20% of this amount, or $1,120. Isn't this great? We've made a profit and have been receiving this annuity-type payment and all we have to claim is $1,120. And it's this large in the first year because of the large down payment! If the principal received next year is, say, $720, then we would have to claim 20% of this amount, or $144. As the principal part of the monthly payment becomes larger, then we'll pay more. Twenty percent will have to be claimed each year. But we'll have twenty-five to thirty years to claim our profit. Interest earned, of course, is a separate issue, and must be claimed as income.

Note: if this property had been held for six months prior to selling it this way, then even the amount claimed would qualify for long-term tax gains treatment. In our example, we'd have to claim 40% of the $1,120. This rate may change each year, but the installment sales ratio will not change.

I realize this is difficult to understand at first, but after you've run through it a couple of times, it will become clear. Then as you understand and use this selling advantage, you'll realize what a great way to sell this is. You could actually create a fortune by "wrapping" properties and paying very little tax because you can claim the gain over the whole course of the loan.

Monthly Income: the next great attribute of carrying paper is the monthly income generated by such a transaction. Money— especially big chunks of it—has a way of disappearing. These monthly payments, though, just keep coming in. Steady monthly income has always been my goal. Just think how nice it will be when you have several perpetual annuity checks in your mailbox every month.

Many people have asked me, "Why not get cash?" I say, "Because cash leaves right away." They ask about the present value and I ask what present or future value there is if the money is gone? One man told me he bought a new Cadillac with a chunk of money he received and then proceeded to tell me that all he had to show for it after a few years was an old Cadillac.

Steady monthly income frees up your life. Ask anybody with payments coming in. I agree, the value of the money may go down, but so does the value of Cadillacs or anything else you may buy with it.

Slow Amortization: the loan doesn't pay off very quickly. As a matter of fact, very little of the monthly payment will come off the principal in the early years. You'll eventually receive a total amount way over the contract price because of all the interest payments.

There are also other reasons. You can create these equity notes and borrow against them, and you don't have to pay taxes on the borrowed funds. Imagine claiming your profits on the installment sales method and borrowing against the note! Now you have that money to invest or spend, or whatever. As you pay it back to the bank, you can deduct the interest you're paying. You could also trade these notes for other things—cars, property, or jewelry. The sky is the limit when you get creative.

Proper Documentation

This method of selling is called a "wraparound." It has become a very popular word, but many people still don't know what it means. It's just a piece of paper that creates a lien (loan) on the property. It is used to leave the existing loans alone. For example, I buy a house for $63,000 with $3,000 down. I assume a loan of $50,000 with a payment of $500 and give the sellers a second mortgage or deed of trust for $10,000 and $100 per month. I put $1,000 into fixing it up and now sell it for $74,000 with $4,000 down. I have received all the money I put in, and now I have a new buyer that owes me $70,000 with payments coming in to me of about $700. I do not let the new buyer assume the existing loans. We leave them intact. We do a wraparound. He owes me $70,000, I owe $60,000. He sends in a payment of $700, and I pay out $600 on the two loans.

Now, I know many of you think that this is complicated, but it just isn't. Hard, yes; complicated, no. I say that it's difficult because it takes a lot of time. Nothing comes easily. Finding the right property to sell quickly obviously is essential to the whole process, but it is being done by thousands of people all over the country. Some real estate offices around the country even have a name for it. They call it "cooking properties" after my last name. I'm grateful that it is working for so many people.

One comment I hear everywhere goes something like this: "Wade, your plan is not easy, but it beats everything else." They say: "Every other book and seminar out there tells us to buy and then rent. We can hardly ever rent the properties for what the payments are, and with your plan, we get higher payments when we sell, more security, and we also get all or most of our down payment back so we can do it again."

That's the whole point. It works because it solves so many problems. You have a need to build cash flow—this plan builds cash flow. You have a need to pay fewer taxes—this plan creates a tax problem, but it's spread out for twenty-five to thirty years because you only have to claim your gain as you receive it. You have a need to maximize the return on your investment, and if done properly, you have no cash in. You put it in, get it out, create a note.

My average net monthly payment is about $195 per month. I have one that was $8 and one $290, but the average is just under $200. Most people can do this twenty or thirty times and retire. Just one property a month means that in two years, it's golf time. If you can do more, and most people do after they get familiar with it, so much the better.

By the way, most people think I'm crazy when I talk about doing something this quickly. But remember what Malcolm Forbes said, "No success is ever accomplished by a reasonable man." Besides, it sure is a lot more fun to go at something with intensity than to sit around and be bored.

Let me show you what I mean with the following story (the New England states have a few obstacles to overcome in this as well as in any other plan. Some attorneys do everything and take their time about it. Out West we can buy and sell in the same day, and escrow and title companies do everything).

I was in Buffalo last August. An elderly lady kept fidgeting in her chair in the middle of the room. It got quite annoying, and I finally asked her if she was okay. She said, "I just have to say something. You were here in May, and after listening to you, I thought you sounded a little nuts, but you looked like a nice guy, so I went out Sunday afternoon and found a little house I could buy. I didn't know how, so I went to an attorney on Monday morning and told him I wanted to buy it that day. He said okay, but it would take three weeks or so to close. I told him that I wanted it done in a few hours, that a man named Wade Cook said that it could be done that quickly and, if not, to shut up and get busy." The audience chuckled at this point.

She continued: "The attorney said that it would take three weeks. He'd been an attorney for eighteen years, and it would just take that long. I told him that it wasn't good enough, but to prove his point he called the title company to have them tell me it takes longer. They told him they weren't busy and could do it that morning. We did it by noon. Now, Mr. Cook, you told me I could do it in one day, and you also said I could resell it right away. I knew I had a good deal, so I went to a real estate office and asked if they had anyone who wanted to buy a house. They did. We waited until 3:00 P.M. when this man got off work to show it. They wanted the house. We went back to the same attorney, and his partner helped us wrap up the whole thing by five o'clock. I'm making $82 per month now for eighteen years, then it goes up to $412 for the last ten years."

Everyone in the audience was staring at this woman. She finished, "I've done it eleven more times in the last four months, and I'm making $1,080 per month, net."

I, too, was impressed, but her story is very common. My mailbox is full of similar stories, but hers was exceptional. I then asked her if she would mind telling us her age. She said, "I'm seventy-two."

Don Berman said it best, "You can make money or you can make excuses, but you can't make both."

There are people all over the country making what I did look like child's play. The concept is simple. Instead of going for the cash, we go for the cash flow. I was standing in the back of a seminar room in San Jose, waiting to be introduced. A young man came up and thinking he recognized me from my picture asked if I was Wade Cook. When I said I was, he told me a very common story.

He told me he had gone to a seminar that teaches many ways to buy real estate but nothing else. He bought two properties and had a negative cash flow each month of $600. He said, "I read your book, and two days later I sold them and now have a positive income of $500 each month."

If there is one thing that I want to be known for it is cash flow. When I die, I want my epitaph to be "Wade Cash-Flow Cook."

Letters come in from all over—testimonials to the fact that a simple plan done persistently will bring results, big results, if you work at it in a big way. A man in Kansas is now the regional director for the western half of the state for the Boy Scouts of America after following this plan for ten months and freeing up his time with steady monthly income.

A woman in Syracuse is up to twenty-eight properties and has made $284,256 in about ten months. Another woman in Baton Rouge had $3,000 left from a life insurance policy on her husband, who had died a few years before. She had never purchased property before but now did so 30 times in ten months. She has over $3,000 a month coming in, and this amount will increase for her and for everyone else when the underlying loans start to pay off.

I could go on and on, but you get the point. It works in Watts and on Long Island. From Seattle to Miami. The letters keep coming in.

If you put down $2,000 and get it back a week later (or a month later) and have created a mortgage with an income stream, your rate of return is infinity because you can't even measure it. You can't divide by zero. If you are lucky and find one for no money down and make $10,000 next year, you're at infinity again. If you learn how to refinance when purchasing and free up money when you buy (which is tax-deferred, by the way), once again you're at infinity or better. When I hear all of these people talking about a 28% return or a 100% return or even 150%, I say, "Don't talk to me about anything less than infinity."

CHAPTER 11

Negotiate Good Deals

The virtues of real estate can be extolled endlessly, but nothing happens until offers are made. You could even meet an agent and look at properties or call on ads in the paper, but it takes an offer to get the ball rolling. But there are not many Henry Kissingers in the world. Most of us are afraid to negotiate. Negotiating is selling. It's selling an idea, or an interest rate, or even yourself.

You perfect your abilities by doing. Many times I've been rejected and, driving away, I've said to myself, "Why did you say that, Wade? That's so dumb. No wonder they didn't like the offer," but I hope that I haven't made the same mistake twice. Practice makes perfect.

Many other good books have been written on negotiating. Read all you can. One book is by an investor, Roger Dawson, entitled *You Can Get Anything You Want,* and dwells a lot on real estate.

I really appreciate those people who write me letters. Some of the letters thank me for my books, but most describe success stories about properties they have purchased. But they didn't purchase them and make the money they did by reading a book. It takes a phone call or a knock on a door and putting it all on a piece of paper to get the deal underway.

Negotiating Can Be Learned

Negotiating in real estate or in any other profession is a learned experience. None of us are born negotiators. However, there is no reason that you can't be a good negotiator. Negotiation will open the door for you to buy cheaper, sell better, and do so in an expeditious manner. Let's clarify something right now about negotiating. There is a big difference between negotiation and manipulation. Often when we hear about someone negotiating a real estate deal, we find ourselves thinking that perhaps this person got exactly what he wanted and the other party came out with nothing. I consider that manipulation. This is not our goal. To be a good negotiator requires that you help the people on the other side of the bargaining table attain their desires as well as you attaining yours. If this sounds a little like the Golden Rule, you're right. Once I met a woman who desperately wanted to move out of her home. Her husband had died six years before, and the house had steadily deteriorated. She had a teenage daughter, and together they found a nice apartment with a swimming pool. I told her that her price for the house was too low. She said, "I know. I could fix this and that and get it up in value, but I don't want to. I hate this place and want out. I'm half moved now. Just give me $800 and promise me I won't have to worry about the back payments, and it's yours." We drew up the papers and she left satisfied. For the first time in a long time, she could relax and enjoy life.

She wanted only to get out and didn't want anything down, but I didn't feel right about that. I put myself in her shoes and felt that $800 was fair. She was thankful for this, and I was glad that we *both* got what we wanted. It is my contention that following the Golden Rule in negotiating will allow an investor to sleep at night with a clear conscience.

Negotiation is just another term for creativity. If you will just make up your mind to negotiate, or to be creative, you will automatically negotiate better deals. Decide before you ever start investing that you are going to try it. Take a few risks, and it will add spice to your investing.

People are intelligent. When I first started investing, I thought that perhaps I could learn something about a property that the seller didn't know. This might be true in terms of potential or my tax advantages, but it is rarely true in terms of present value or current rent prices. After my first deal, I dispelled that notion and started hoping for really intelligent people to do business with. It was with these people that I prospered, and I'm confident that they did too. This concept will ensure success.

Times have changed. The economy has changed. But people haven't changed, and neither have their needs. People need security and monthly income buys that security. In today's marketplace, if we look past the high interest rates and advertised prices and look at the basic reason that real estate is such a good investment, we will see that the disadvantages created by today's economy can, in turn, create advantages for those of us seeking monthly income from real estate.

What has happened is that the same set of facts that might make a property seem out of reach actually creates a set of facts that makes it an even better investment in terms of leverage, tax shelters, and control of appreciation.

Let's get specific and buy a four-plex for $100,000, a purchase you will want to approach with some caution. You want to maximize your cash, so you offer a lower price with less down and at a lower interest rate. The lower down aspect lets you leverage higher and, consequently, the leveraged cost of your tax benefits, equity appreciation, and income is enhanced. Now is not the time to back off and wait. It is the time to turn disadvantages into advantages.

Solutions to these types of problems are as varied as the problems themselves. The owner wants to sell, you want to buy, along comes a little negotiation and creativity, and a purchase is made. Let's get down to some negotiating tips that you can use today in your investing.

I've always found it advantageous when I'm negotiating with people to take along a yellow legal pad. Most of the time my negotiating is done on the floor in a vacant house. By using the pad, I can write things down. I prefer to use a bold felt-tip pen rather than a normal ballpoint pen. I write down my offer, and they change the offer by taking the pad from me and scratching out what they didn't like. There can be no misunderstandings this way. What I write down is completely understood. There are times when $50,000 can sound like $15,000, and in verbalizing there is always a chance of misunderstanding. Not so when things are put down on paper. It is very wise to do all of your negotiating with paper and pen in hand so that everybody can see what's going on.

Carry Legal Forms and Deeds

Along with your yellow legal pad, it is a good idea to carry all necessary deeds and contracts with you. If for no other reason, carry them to show the people what they will have to sign at the closing. It would also be helpful to be familiar with these forms. If people ask you questions, the answers are often on the forms themselves. For example, when I've made offers, I would often be asked how the seller would be protected, since I always use the Money Machine method of owner-financing. They wanted to know what would happen if I didn't make the payments to them, or if I sold the house to someone who didn't make the payments to them. I simply pulled out the legal forms and showed them these provisions, which were standard, legal, and in writing. This would always ease their fears. It's also nice to know this information for your own benefit. Legal forms have inherent credibility.

Along with these two tangible negotiating tips, there are a few intangible tips that you should know before you start negotiating on any specific deal.

Negotiate Only In Good Condition

As reported in *Barter News:*

> Negotiators in good physical and mental condition have an obvious advantage over those who went without sleep, who have been drinking, who haven't eaten properly for a day and a half, or who

are distracted by others. Turn any disadvantages to your advantage. You should always be in top form when negotiating. While an experienced negotiator who is tired may make a better deal than an inexperienced person, the experienced, alert negotiator has an advantage over a similarly experienced negotiator whose brain is dulled or whose body is tired. If you are not at your best, postpone the negotiations or have another good negotiator/investor do it for you.

Find Out Why People Are Selling

People sell properties for many good reasons. It's important to find out the "why" behind their selling. You won't be able to offer alternatives until you know what is needed. A friend of mine made an offer on a house that required $2,000 down, which was more than he wanted to put into it.

Upon inquiring why that much was needed, he found out that the seller wanted to get his daughter a car for about $1,000. My friend quickly offered his wife's car, which the man took as credit for $1,000. His wife was angry for a few weeks, until he sold the house and bought her a newer station wagon, which she loved. He also made enough to get two more houses.

Don't Come Across As A Wheeler-Dealer

If a person comes across as a wheeler-dealer, it could be a great detriment in the negotiating process. For instance, if an investor is sitting there with all of his pat answers and every time the owner states a problem or something he needs and the investor hardly lets the owner finish his sentence, then interrupts him and comes back with another quick solution, it could be too much razzle-dazzle for the seller. One of the ways to avoid this is to realize that people are not going to feel satisfied until they feel understood. Let me illustrate.

A man had a friend who was an optometrist. He made an appointment for a checkup to see if he needed glasses. He walked into the optometrist's office and the optometrist listened to the man talk a little bit about his problems. Then the optometrist said, "I've been wearing these glasses for nine years, and they have sure done a good job for me. Why don't you take these glasses and wear them?"

The man took the optometrist's glasses and put them on, saying, "I still see things a little blurry."

The optometrist replied, "Oh, you'll get used to that. My eyes were blurred a little in the beginning, but you'll get used to the new glasses."

The man wore the glasses for a few weeks and still couldn't see well and started getting headaches. He went back to the optometrist and stated that he needed to get a new pair of glasses.

Now, obviously, if this had actually happened, we would call it absurd because we wouldn't take any kind of prescription or recommendation like that without the proper analysis of the problem for our own eyes.

The point is that until sellers feel that we understand their problems, we might come across as someone who is trying to take advantage of them. Over a period of time (usually hours), by digging into and understanding their problems, these wheeler-dealer thoughts and appearances will disappear. When they feel that we understand them, they will be more receptive to our offer.

Show Understanding

Understanding is the watchword. Understand the seller's problems. Understand your goals. Understand the process of lining up these two things. The following are a few lessons I learned that helped me be creative and get the job done. I think they will be of value to you in your negotiations.

First, people do things for *their* reasons, not yours. This was taught to me best when I was selling a house. I had used bank loans to extensively repair the house. Everything was remodeled inside and out! New carpet, drapes, paint, roof, landscaping, cabinets, fireplace, and so on. I was so proud when it was completed, and I wasn't a bit surprised when it sold the next day. After negotiating the deal, I asked the woman what had made her buy it. My chest was six inches bigger while waiting for her answer, but then it deflated when she said, "I've always wanted a double stainless steel kitchen sink." That was probably the only thing in the house I hadn't repaired or replaced. If you want to negotiate a sale or purchase, it is vital to ascertain the motives of the other person.

Second, people act in their best interests. Often when I was investing and buying and processing up to six properties a month, I found that the first reason given was actually not the "whole truth and nothing but the truth." I'm not saying that anyone deliberately lied to me, but I learned quickly that most people are very intelligent. The closer the problem gets to home (their home), the more intelligent and cautious they become. Good! That's the way it should be. If some people think that they'll get rich by running around taking advantage of unsuspecting people, they have a powerful lesson to learn.

I have watched many people who thought they could circumvent the law of honesty. They cannot and did not: we *always* reap what we sow. It got to the point where I would rather do business with a sophisticated person. When we both understood what was in each other's best interest, a deal was made.

Third, people will not trade their certainties. If you're proposing an unfamiliar concept, then you'll have to spend extra time educating the seller. This will be time well spent if the seller ends up feeling good about you and your offer. Remember to carry legal forms to help assuage any fears.

For example, you meet the sellers, and even though they don't know you from Adam, you make them an offer to pay them a little money two years from now, then start payments to them after that time. And you also want to secure this amount against another property later on, a property that they don't know from the Garden of Eden. Do you wonder that they'll be apprehensive?

This principle carries over to selling your property as well. If a family has $5,000 in the bank for a down payment on a house and the house you have to sell is surrounded with questions, they most likely won't buy it. Let's suppose the bathroom needs some work. That's simple enough, but maybe all kinds of things are going through their minds. How long will it take? How much will it cost? Who can we get to fix it up? There are answers to these questions, but sometimes that doesn't matter. With too many questions, it's easier for them to find another house to buy than yours. Be ready with answers, but first eliminate those things that make people uneasy.

Financing poses another kind of uncertainty. Obviously, most sellers want to get as much down or as high a monthly payment as possible. These terms leave many questions in the buyer's mind, especially with the economic climate the way it is. They don't know if they'll have a job next year, or what happens if their wife gets pregnant and has to quit work?

In order to alleviate many of those questions, you should be aware of them and take as much uncertainty out of the sale as possible. When explaining the financing terms, write it down on your legal pad so the figures are recognizable and can eliminate error.

If you put a house for sale in the newspaper and don't specifically list the terms, people cannot be sure whether you're charging 10, 11, or 15% for your interest rate. They're also uncertain what the monthly payments will be or how much the taxes are. When it is time to start bargaining, they don't know where to start because there are too many uncertainties. If they have $2,000 in their checking account to put down on a house, they are afraid to trade their $2,000 for a house that represents too many uncertainties, even though it may be a good deal.

A good rule to remember is that the way to eliminate uncertainties in your negotiations is to keep asking yourself questions that they might ask: "Would I want this deal?" "Do I understand these terms?" Houses are purchased to solve people's problems. Have as many solutions on hand as possible.

Figure 11-1

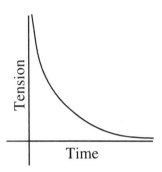

Fourth, tension is lessened with time. The longer you can spend with the seller, the better the relationship becomes. This is best described by looking at figure 11-1.

When first meeting with no time elapsed at all, the tension is high. As time progresses, the tension is lessened. I'm not advocating spending hours talking about the weather, but there are many things that can be discussed that will uncover mutual areas of interest and build rapport. Later, many things you've discussed will be helpful in your negotiations.

There will be times when several meetings will be needed over a period of days or weeks. That's okay. Inexperienced negotiators lose patience too quickly to conclude the deal. Keep going back. The result is worth it, not to mention the new friend you'll have.

Fifth, ask a lot of questions to avoid surprises. Use a property analysis form (found at the end of this book) or questionnaire and fill it out completely. If this form is filled out properly and you have all the information, you are in a position to create a Golden Rule deal. The reason I say "all the information" is that many times I would get to a closing only to find one more encumbrance that the seller forgot about, or that the interest rate and payment that I was assuming was not exactly what it was supposed to be.

It's no fun to have surprises in the investing business. To ensure that you don't have any surprises after you make your offer, ask questions such as these:

"Mr. Jones, can we go over your file and make sure we haven't missed anything?"

"Did you take out any other loans while you owned this property?"

"Might there be any other liens from suits, divorces, car accidents, or whatever else you can think of?"

Stay a step ahead by having all the information.

I use a very simple property analysis sheet that is on the front and back of an $8^1/_2$ x 11 piece of paper. It can be filled out in about five minutes, and it takes about that long to make a decision because only the pertinent financial information is listed. It's called a "Property Analysis Sheet," and is found at the back of this book.

Sixth, be prepared with several alternatives. These shouldn't be presented like: "Well, you don't like this one; how about this one?" Instead, use one alternative as a springboard for another: "Well, would this work if we did this instead of that?" To get the job done, you almost have to be a pharmacist with a pill for every ill.

Seventh, be creative and persistent. Creativity is not some magic formula that brings success and happiness. I know several people who were considered creative by everyone because they put together deals no one else could, or because they bought over $5 million worth of real estate.

Close inspection of the methods of operation of these successful investors shows something that is always left out in the writeups: that something is the persistence that went into their success. Sure, they made a good deal, but do you realize that it's been two months and 18 other rejected earnest monies before they got this one? They work sixty hours a week! The deals are there, but with buying and selling, you have to play a numbers game. When the final tally is taken, the investors and negotiators who are successful are the persistent ones.

Tangible Negotiations

Now that you are armed with some of the emotions involved in negotiating, it's time to get down to brass tacks. What exactly do you say to sellers to get them to come to a mutually beneficial agreement with you?

Cash Or Nothing Down?

There are many properties out there that can be purchased with little or no money down. It may not seem so at first because they don't stick out. You have to dig in and find them. Maybe your hometown doesn't have many opportunities, but there are communities all over this country with many good deals.

Don't ever mention to sellers that you're trying to buy their property with nothing down. Instead, tell them about the other benefits, such as the tax benefits of selling on contract or the benefits of monthly payments. To sellers, price is more important than terms; to buyers, terms are more important than price.

As stated earlier in the book, when you start the negotiating process, agree only to pay cash as a last resort. Don't tell the sellers you have any; tell them you need it for fixing up the property. Maybe you can tell them (and ease their fears about you at the same time) that your successes have brought on a tax liability and you need your money for that, or that you need their property for other tax write-offs.

Give Them What They Want

Sellers may ask you to agree to some terms that you do not find agreeable. You must recognize these requests as trade-offs and not as something you are going to give away. The sellers may ask you to do something that you view as simple and you agree. Later on, when you ask for something "simple," they may not view it the same way and will refuse. If you recognize this as a trade-off situation, you will be able to maximize their requests to your benefit. Have a list of concessions that you want before you start negotiating. Then when they ask for a concession, you can ask them for one in return. When you are asked for a major or minor concession, don't just say yes and rush on to the big items of negotiation. Instead, trade the give-up for a concession you want. "Sure, I'll buy the house before you fix the roof, if you'll knock $1,000 off the purchase price."

Remember the example about the man who gave his wife's car as part of a down payment? I call this "giving them what they want, but in a different way."

In almost every purchase I have made, the sellers wanted cash to pay off some obligation. Sometimes they needed it for repair work on other properties. You can assume many obligations and have the repair work done, sometimes at a fraction of the cost that they will pay for it.

Here are several examples:

- One woman needed $3,000 to put a new roof on her mother's house. I put it on for $1,600 and got credit for the $3,000 to buy her rental unit.

- One man needed $2,000 for some landscaping. I had it done by finding a landscaper who took a mortgage and note payable at $50 a month against the property.

- One man needed $2,200 to pay the back property taxes. In my state, nothing happens until they are five years' delinquent. Then all one needs to do is pay only for the fifth year back. It cost me nothing to get the money off his back.

Ask Open-Ended Questions

Ask open-ended questions and see what you can discover. Many investors have a business in which products or services can be readily traded or bartered. The format for trading can be in the form of a scrip, which is a piece of paper, or a certificate, drawn up with a value on it and with an expiration date for its use. This scrip can be taken out and traded for a down payment.

For example, if you own a tire repair company, you may make up $50 scrip. If you made up one hundred of them, you would have $5,000 in scrip, which you could trade for other goods or services that you need done on your properties, or you could trade it for a down payment. The scrips are transferrable: they may be taken and given to someone else. The sellers of the property that you're trying to buy will take scrip for tires, dental work, medical services, or others. They may use part of them or trade part of them to other people for cash. The possibilities are limitless. You do not need to own a business to deal in scrip. In fact, you can go into a business and offer to buy products at a discounted rate and actually buy scrip that you could trade at full market value.

Sometimes in the negotiating process, you might be stalled with possible solutions to the sellers' problems. If you are stalled or are up against the wall, one of the best things to do is ask the sellers "Do you have any solutions? Do you have any other way that we could handle structuring my purchase of this house that would be beneficial to both of us?"

You might want to plant some seeds, using these questions. For instance, ask a question like this, "Can you think of any other assets that you or I might have that could be included in this transaction, possibly something that could be sold to come up with the cash that we need in order to put this deal together?"

Let me give an example that one of my seminar attendees told me about some years ago. I teach this concept in my seminars, and he had a set of my tapes. He was from New York and was driving in northern New Jersey. The property he saw was near the ocean and had a simple FOR SALE sign in the front yard. He stopped and looked: five acres, with a rather large house and a large garden area in the rear with plants, trees, and bushes everywhere.

The asking price through an estate sale was $110,000. He offered $10,000 down and the balance within one year. No payments at all. He also put in an escape clause to get out of the deal within three weeks because he didn't have the $10,000. But after listening to my story about a man buying two lots in Oregon and selling the timber from one to own the other free and clear, he contacted a nursery and they offered close to $12,000 for much of the greenery. He used this money for the down payment.

He then put it up for sale and with not one dime into fixing it up, sold it and closed on the deal six weeks later for $135,000. The new sellers got a loan, and after closing costs, he put $31,000 in his pocket ($135,000 minus the $100,000 obligation minus $4,000 in closing costs). A handsome profit for about ten hours of work. And his story is not unusual. I hear of similar experiences everywhere I go. He would not have made one dime, though, had he not stopped the car and started talking.

If questions are asked in such a way as to lead the sellers into thinking about new solutions rather than just answering yes or no, which is the answer to a closed question, the seller's imagination is sparked and led into a direction where he/she might come up with a different set of circumstances that might be mutually beneficial.

One further note on this subject: it is very hard to carry on this kind of conversation with the seller if there are one or two agents doing the negotiating for you. If there is a piece of property that you really want and agents are involved, you might want to use all the finesse you have to see that you sit down with the seller. Once agents are trained to represent you the way you think best, then they can be on their own. At first, though, you should be present if for no other reason than to educate the agent. Even if the agents are there, a better conversation will ensue because you can look each other in the eye, sit and discuss things, and put things on paper.

Wording The Deal

Many times in talking with people, they will hear what they want to hear—which may not be exactly what you're saying. If sellers want cash and are willing to wait a short period of time for it but need your assurance that you're going to pay it off as quickly as you can, they should get the assurance in writing. To protect yourself while letting them know that you're trying hard to meet their demands, you may want to look at the wording you're using in your earnest money agreement to reach the goals you both have.

For example, if you promise to pay the sellers $1,000 in a year, and you use the words "in a year," they might think that they will get the money at the end of one year from the time you're talking to them. However, if you use the words "within a year," it sounds better to them. They're hearing that they may get their money *before* the end of the year. It means exactly the same thing to you: you still have a year to come up with the $1,000.

Sometimes people think that they will not be able to enforce the terms of the contract, or maybe the implication of certain words are more in the buyer's favor than in theirs. The normal wording in an earnest money agreement and contract could be changed to make them much more comfortable. For example, "It is mandatory that the purchasers make this monthly payment on the due date. If not they will have to pay a late charge of $15." Compare that to: "A $15 late payment will be assessed if payment is not received on or before the due date." Yes, they do both say exactly the same thing, but the first one sounds a lot more comfortable to the seller.

Summary

Constantly look at houses, and the deals will be there. Of course, you won't be able to get compatible terms on every house. If you can't, be prepared to move on to the next deal. There's always another deal around the corner. When a good deal starts to become mediocre, you must be willing to walk. But don't give up. Some of the most profitable deals ever made are made immediately after things look darkest, or after an outright refusal. But if you're creative and persistent, your negotiations will pay off, and you'll make good deals where others can't.

CHAPTER 12

GET THE LOW DOWN ON REAL ESTATE

In the last chapter, we discussed negotiating. Just as nothing happens until a written offer is made, an offer won't be accepted until it solves and meets the needs of the sellers. Until they feel understood and satisfied, they will not agree to anything. The only time that this is not true is when they are desperate and will do anything to unload their property. Although this doesn't happen every day, it does happen often enough for investors to find some really good deals. Once again, I don't want to take advantage of anybody, but I would rather have the property than see the bank get it back.

Robert G. Allen, in his book *Nothing Down,* made the phrase "Don't Wanter," famous, and this concept is worth discussing here before we get into a few specific techniques for purchasing real estate with very little down.

If some people want to sell their property more than I want to buy, I can probably structure a good deal. If I want to buy more than they want to sell, then they are in control. Finding these good deals is simply a numbers game or a matter of luck. You can't control luck, but you can play the numbers game. Can you control the game? Let's explore it.

We've all heard something like this from various businesses, "I looked at fifteen, made offers on six, and bought one." The numbers could vary, but the concept is the same. You cannot control the one, all you can control is the fifteen. The one is a by-product of the fifteen.

Everywhere there are people who really need to sell. They may be across town or around the corner, but they're there. You are not going to get a great low-down deal on every property. Don't get discouraged, play the game. Figure out how many, or how large a property you want to buy and go for it.

The reason I bring this up is because as I give several ways to buy with low down, you'll be thinking, "that won't work on the green house on Elm Street," and you're probably right. I don't have a pill for every ill in every case. Anyway, if you say it won't work, you're right, it won't. Your attitude will make or break most deals. For example, later on in this chapter I'll mention three educational techniques to show the seller how great it is to take monthly payments instead of cash. I was teaching in St. Louis, and the real estate editor from the *Globe Democrat* was there. He listened to my seminar and later, when he interviewed me, he said, "Your enthusiasm for monthly payments probably causes more people to accept them than the actual technique." I submit the same to you: enthusiasm makes things happen.

Enough theory, let's get into the specifics. Several techniques will be given. You will probably use only one at a time, even though a combination of ways sometimes will save a sinking deal. These techniques are taken from my book *101 Ways To Buy Real Estate Without Cash*. No one needs 101 ways, but that is how many ways and relative techniques are given. This is so that readers can pick a few that feel comfortable and get good at applying them. It reminds me of the guy who knew eighty-nine ways to make love but didn't know any girls.

If some people want cash for their equity, and most people probably do, then I have two choices: either I get them the money or I change their mind. Every seminar and every book written on the subject teaches techniques that fall under one of these categories. A combination is possible perhaps in a situation where we give them some cash and change their mind on the rest.

Total Owner Carryback

This way is my favorite. Not every seller can do it, but it's always my first offer. Example: a duplex for $63,000 has an existing loan of $50,000 FHA. I offer to take over the loan and give the seller a mortgage for $13,000 at $130 per month. The offer probably won't be accepted, but it's a place to start.

When you go into any transaction and start to negotiate, be very careful to make sure that your offer is not only reasonable but possibly even lower than where you think is reasonable so that as you start making your offer better, you can bring it up to where it should be or where you think it's most beneficial to you.

For example, I had a client who called me from Philadelphia who had found a tremendous deal on a four-plex. He wanted to buy it. The price was about fifty cents on the dollar for the valuation of the units, and he really wanted them. The price was $40,000, and the value was $80,000. The existing financing included an assumable loan of $20,000. I asked him how the seller wanted his equity; and, of course, he said that the seller wanted cash.

I asked, "What would you like to pay?"

He said, "I'd like to pay him his $20,000 in two years."

I said, "Okay, that might not be too bad, but why do you want to do that?"

He said, "Well, that's one of the techniques I learned at a seminar."

I said, "That's a good technique, but do you really want to do that? Do you really want to be responsible for coming up with $20,000 two years from now?"

He said, "No."

I said, "Then how about if we ask him to take $200 a month for his $20,000?" My client really liked this idea. Then I asked him, "Do you really want to pay him $200 a month?"

He said, "No."

Then I said, "Well, why don't we ask him if we can start making his $200 payments two years from now?"

He said, "Yeah, that sounds good."

I asked, "But do you really want to pay him $200 a month beginning two years from now?"

He said, "No."

I said, "Then, why don't we start payments two years from now of $100 a month for a year and then we'll raise it to $150 a month for a year and then we'll raise it to $200 for the balance of the loan."

He really liked this idea, and that's what we put into the earnest money agreement.

Obviously, when he walks in with this offer, he's going to hit the seller right between the eyes with it. But several things were accomplished here. One of them is that he is starting low enough to come up to something that would be comfortable both to him and to the seller. The important point is that he is not only starting where he would be comfortable, but he is starting below where he would be comfortable.

The second point is that no matter what, the offer is going to start the negotiating process. The purpose of negotiating and discussing what the seller can afford to take and what the buyer can afford to give is to make sure that both of them come out on the same foot—that they're both standing there and both understand exactly what the other can afford. Now that they have this understood, they are prepared to make an application of what they've learned. This application might be to walk out the door because no deal can be made; or the application might be to sit down and fill out an earnest money agreement and have a deal put together.

One final note on this idea: do not be afraid to ask questions or to offer something that you think might be embarrassing. Because what might be embarrassing to you might be totally acceptable to the seller. So make sure that you figure out where you want to be, and sometimes the crazier the better.

Lump Sum in the Future

One of the easiest ways to buy is give the sellers exactly what they want (or close to it) but give it to them later. Back to our $63,000 property. They want their $13,000 equity in cash. Give it to them in two, five, or 10 years from now. Obviously, the longer the better. We will probably have to pay an interest rate on this amount, which will just accrue. When we pay it off, it could be $15,000 or higher, but that's okay. The property has probably gone up in value. We get the growth on everything, they get interest only on their loan amount.

How else do we benefit? Our payments are lower right now. If I'm going to give someone a balloon payment, the trade-off is usually no payments or very low payments in the meantime.

Combination

Let's say our sellers need some cash. They're willing to take monthly payments on part of their equity, but they have a need for some money. The trap here is that we might give more than we should. We get excited about getting monthly payments and then agree to too much down—$63,000, as before, but this time they want $6,000 down. That's just under 10% of the purchase price, and though it sounds good, let's not stop here. Let's counter back at $3,000. Once again, we will assume the $50,000 and now give them a $10,000 mortgage for the balance at $100 per month.

In both cases I've offered a monthly payment of 1% of the mortgage amount. If the payment was on the whole $63,000, it would be $630 per month. I'm not terribly concerned about the length of time to pay off the loan. I'm concerned about the affordability of the property. The 1% repayment factor is just a good target.

It would be well to take this affordability factor one step further. I not only want to get monthly payments, but in today's economy I'd like to get graduated monthly payments. That simply means the payments will increase for a few years. I'm not talking about an ARM (Adjustable Rate Mortgage), or any of its cousins. I'm talking about a simple concept that allows us to make a profit from day one.

Using the same example, let's assume that the payment on the $50,000 FHA is $520, which amount includes PITI (Principal, Interest, Taxes, and Insurance). The property will rent for $540, hopefully. If we pay out $100 on a second mortgage, our payments total $620 and we'll lose $80 per month, and this doesn't include repairs and maintenance.

If we want to make a profit, let's try this: "The purchaser agrees to pay $20 per month the first year. The payment will then increase $20 per month each year on [date] for seven years to $160 per month and remain at $160 for the remainder of the loan." You'll notice we're even giving more than the $100 but it will take us seven years to get to that level. And we get to make a profit in the meantime. If rents go up at 5%, we'll make $25 extra per month per year.

I don't even buy properties unless I can get graduated payments. One other point: most of us are in this for keeps. We're creating long-term income. If we do not learn how to get low payments now, we'll go out of business. Those investors who are alive and well and happy with their investments are those who have learned to get low payments up front so they can get and keep their profits.

By the way, this last purchase information is so common that it alone makes a case for the Money Machine concept when an investor first starts out. We could sell it and get a higher payment, and, if we do sell, we can now give a better deal to the new buyer by giving him graduated payments. One man in Atlanta buys properties for $50,000 at 10% and $480 per month and sells them for $50,000 at 11 1/2% interest at $550 per month. I've never done anything this close, but it can be done.

Cash for Equity

Before we get into the ideas for finding ways to give the sellers something other than cash for their equity, let's lay a proper foundation.

In almost all types of real estate transactions currently taking place, the property has some type of financing or liens against it.

The owners trying to sell it will only get out their equity, which is the difference between their selling price or the value of the property, and the loans that exist against it. If the loans are assumable, then the most common approach that the owners take is to get cash for their equity.

This can be accomplished in many ways. Most owners do not particularly care if their property is totally refinanced or their loans are assumed. If the loans are assumable, there are several ways to come up with the money. It can be borrowed from a bank, it can be used out of your personal savings, it could be borrowed from a friend or partner. The more cash you use should mean the better the deal.

The major concern, though, is that you fully understand and have a grasp of what is going to happen to those underlying loans. The owners might think that their loan is assumable. They might also think that the due-on-sale clause or any increase in interest rates or monthly payments will not affect their sale to you. They might feel that their loan was made before the banks got sticky a few years ago about interest rate "sensitivity." It would be wise for people buying a piece of property to know exactly what's going to happen.

If there are clauses existing on the loan documents that are against the property, there are several things that can happen. The first is that the new buyers should not only find out what the bank is going to do, but they should also get it down in writing. For instance, if the present interest rate is 10% and the bank says it is going to raise the rate to 12% and the current monthly payment is $500, and the bank then says it is going to raise it to $570, the changes may or may not be something that the new buyers can live with, but they should have that in writing. Far too often, the buyer will walk in to the bank and talk to the loan officer. The loan officer will say something to the effect that the bank is going to raise the interest rates to 12% and the monthly payments to $570. Three or four weeks later, when the property is actually in closing and the assumption papers come from the bank, they'll find out that the interest rate has been raised to 14%

and the monthly payments are $650. The reasoning from the bank is that what the loan officer quoted when the prospective buyers were in the bank, was what the bank was going to do at that current time that day. But because several weeks have passed, the policies have changed, and the loan committee has come out with new rates that are going to be charged. Get in writing exactly what the bank is going to do.

If the underlying financing is through an individual, and if the contract the current owners have signed does not mention resale or assumption conditions, then you can almost rest assured that there will not be any changes. The original lender may try, however.

Almost all loans, in all states, are assumable under the conditions that currently exist. That is why the banks have done so much changing in recent years: to make sure that they are protected, to cover themselves for any kind of contingencies. There's one more point here. The due-on-sale clause is a sticky subject in many states. Many states, either through legislation or the courts, have virtually eliminated the clause and have even clouded the bank's ability to make payment adjustments. But in some states these clauses in the contract remain intact. They cause unbelievable problems for people who are trying to assume these loans.

Then the problem is really compounded when overzealous buyers or sellers think that they can pull a fast one, or a quick one, on the bank by possibly selling it to somebody and not recording the contract. They'll even go to such extremes as to get double insurance policies so the bank doesn't know that there's a new buyer on the loan. It is *highly recommended* not to play these types of games. The banks are in this money game for keeps. They're in it to win. If they find out that some kind of shenanigans like this are going on, they will call a loan due a lot quicker than if the buyer and seller approached the bank to find out what it was going to do. So the advice is, don't play games. Be out in the open and let everybody know what's going on. If the loans are not assumable according to their conditions, fine, move on to another piece of property.

Let's bring up another point now. The banks, wanting to protect themselves, have thrown in all of those little clauses that have literally placed them out of touch with reality. I have had several clients who purchased property and now, several years later, when they go to sell the property, are informed by the banks that there is a nonassumption agreement; or that they will call the loan due if they sell the property.

I had one client, in particular, who had a $45,000 mortgage. He put his house up for sale for "$10,000 and take over my payments." Interest rates being as high as they then were, he could hardly find anybody who wanted to live in his house in that part of town who could qualify for the $700 a month payment required on a loan for $55,000, (this represented a fair market value for his house). Time after time he approached the bank to see if it would allow the new purchaser to assume the loan. The purchaser seemed qualified, but the bank was trying to get its money back in. I don't understand these banks sometimes. Apparently they were trying to get back in good standing with their up-line banks, but they started acting in their own worst interest.

This buyer tried for a long time to sell his house. He had to move to Little Rock and had already left, but had to leave his family at the old house until it sold. He got tired of being away from them, and after three or four months, he could not afford two house payments.

The unsold house went into a state of foreclosure. He was foreclosed on after a few more months, and the bank ended up with the house. The $450 payment is no longer coming into the bank. After more than a year, they had not found anybody to buy the house; no one could qualify at the new loan rates.

I know for certain that this man had two or three different people at different times who were qualified enough to take over the loan according to the bank's basic standards, except for the fact that they wanted to call the loan due and wouldn't allow any assumption.

This brings up an interesting situation. It can be brought to the bank's attention that the owner is going to have a hard time and that they might end up with the house back. If the bank is not worried about that, then no amount of arguing is going to change it. If the owner of the house points out that he has a good buyer and the loan can be assumed, and that a modest interest rate and monthly increase is acceptable to the buyer, the bank might go ahead, and probably will go ahead, and allow the loan to be assumed.

The last thing you should do is to be intimidated by the banks. They are either going to change the rates or they are not. There is no harm in asking them what they would do once the loan is assumed. Once again, the caution is to get in writing whatever is said.

Continuing on this subject of cash for equity, I should say that banks are very concerned when people use borrowed money to assume *their* loan. They are concerned with the debt service, meaning the monthly payments, on the new loan. For instance, if people borrow money, they will want to know what the new monthly payments will be. They will add the new monthly payment to the current monthly payments and then use that in determining whether the new buyer is going to be qualified or not.

There are several ways to avoid this type of situation. One would be to put the loan against a different piece of property. In effect, the banks will not know where the money is coming from. They will just know that the seller is getting his cash and their loan is being assumed. Simple and uncomplicated.

Get Them What They Want
We don't have to give them what they want; we can get it for them. It's amazing the variety of things people want: a new roof, a move to California, landscaping on their own home, so they're selling a rental property. Sometimes the property taxes get so delinquent or the repairs so overwhelming that people get discouraged. All of this can be solved without a lot of cash.

Just sit back and think of the ways you could move or pay to have the sellers moved to California. This should start you thinking. Note, though, that these amounts are about what the down payment will be. You'll still have to deal with the balance of their equity and make arrangements to give them monthly payments.

Sweat Equity

If coming up with a down payment is hard to do, one of the first things that you should look into is putting your energy and labor as a down payment. For instance, a typical property that might fit into this classification would be one that needs a lot of work, one that people are driving past and not even stopping to look at because of the huge amount of cosmetic work that needs to be done. If people are enterprising, they may walk into the middle of a tremendous deal.

Let's get specific here. Let's say the property is a four-unit that is really run down. All fixed up, it might be worth $100,000. The owner has it up for sale for $70,000 and is even flexible on that price. The owner would like to get $10,000 down to make sure that whoever is buying the property has something at stake and won't walk away. The earnest money could read that the purchaser agrees to buy the property for $60,000 with $10,000 down. The $10,000 will be in the form of work done, meaning that within a period of time, say six months or a year, 1) there will be a new roof put on, 2) the fence will be repaired and the yard work will be taken care of, 3) all four apartments will receive at least 50% new paint, and 4) that within this period of time new carpeting will be laid and any other general cosmetic work needing to be done will be done. In effect, what we are doing in a situation like this is giving him the assurance he needs with our hard work. Now several things might happen in a case like this. One of them is that the seller is going to say, "Hey, I'm not getting anything out of this, you're doing all of this work and you're getting to deduct the full amount off the price."

The answer to that is, "Yes, we're doing the work and here's how it benefits you. You probably won't be able to sell the building in its present state for anywhere near the price you are asking. Second, we only have so much money to buy the property and fix it up. To get it into better renting position so that we can pay the high payments that you are asking, we, like everyone else, will need our money to do the work. If we take our available cash and put it as a down payment to the owner without having any of the work done, it doesn't do any good in that our money is gone and the place still needs repair work."

The third point is that the seller originally had a $60,000 loan against a property that is now worth exactly, possibly even less, than what we're agreeing to pay for it. But once the work is done and the property does have the $100,000 value justified by comparables in the neighborhood, justified by the rent, justified by any formula or multiplier he wants to use, his loan is now secured by a property that is worth a lot more than the loan is. This has three advantages to him: 1) he can go to sleep at night knowing that we have a lot at stake in making the payments; 2) if he ever wants to use his loan as collateral, and a banker or lender were to drive by the property or have its value appraised against his $60,000, the property will show a lot better and he will have a lot better chance of getting a loan; and 3) now that we have a lot of time and money tied up there is a strong chance that we're going to refinance or sell the property to get our money back. This is called "sweat equity" and is a valuable tool.

Get A Loan

Mr. Jones needs cash and only cash in a hurry.

Sorry I have to do this to you—talking about cash when I should be more creative, but there are a few points that need to be mentioned.

1. From our example, we see that a seller is in desperate need of cash, and, no matter what, cash talks. It talks for the following reasons:

   a) It's hard to come by, and bank financing takes a long time.

b) Finding qualified buyers is getting harder all the time. Your cash qualified you.

c) Mr. Jones is in a hurry—compounding his problem, which means that even though he may not be flexible with his terms, he probably will be with his price. Start low to find the happy ground.

2. The property can be purchased quickly in order to take advantage of the low price, then refinanced at your convenience.

3. It's amazing the concessions the seller will make and the things he will repair (or make compensation for) if he knows the money is only a savings account away.

You're throwing leverage to the wind with all-cash purchases, so the deal should be really right for you to get involved.

In short, cash talks. The more cash you have involved, the better the purchase price. But remember not to leave this kind of deal in the oven too long or the whole kitchen will burn down.

One of the fastest ways to solve the seller's need for cash is for you, the buyer, or him, the seller, to get a loan. With interest rates the way they are, try to get it for the equity only. Don't refinance the whole amount unless it's absolutely necessary. Then shop for the best rates. A buyer's loan would be a second mortgage on the property that is equal to the equity in the home or purchase price minus the first mortgage. A seller's loan would also be a second mortgage in the amount of the purchase price minus the first mortgage amount. This loan will be used as your down payment as you, the buyer, would assume the first and second mortgage or make payments to the seller for the second loan.

203K government backed loans are not available anymore. But some mortgage companies will give a similar loan. FHA Title I Remodel since 1934 is still available. The qualifications are: $25,000—no equity needed, no appraisal, and no inspection before the loan is done.

The concept is important. They'll lower the price for cash. If you have a line of credit or cash lying around, you could make some tremendous deals. Remember, though, that you have to figure out a way to get that cash back and keep it working for you.

Change Their Minds

There are three simple educational ideas I use to help people see the beauty of monthly payments. These are not infallible, but they work if you get there before the people have mentally spent the money. Once again, I don't buy many houses from people who are living in the house or are using it for their personal residence. I buy rental properties. People selling their own residences are usually doing so to move into a bigger house. They need cash so I can't always help them. On the other hand, if the property has been a rental property they may be selling it because all the tax write-offs are gone, or maybe they don't want to mess with tenants anymore. The property might need fixing up and they don't have the money to do it. Whatever the case, the gist of the matter is that they need to sell the house more than I need to buy it. The reverse causes nothing but problems.

First, if they sell their rental house to me and take monthly payments, then they claim their profits as they receive them. It could be twenty years. If they get it all now, it could seriously affect their tax bracket. This point is the hardest to explain. IRS Form 6252 parts 1 and 2 will help them see how much they will have to claim, this year and in future years.

Second, if the seller takes $130 a month from me, that money comes in steadily for umpteen years. If the seller gets cash, it just disappears. People really like steady monthly income. Tell them how much that check in their mailbox will mean, every month of every year for the next twenty years. If they argue that $130 won't buy much in twenty years, then remind them that $10,000 spent and gone now won't buy anything.

Third, the fact is that if you buy a house for $80,000 and get a thirty-year mortgage, you will pay over $240,000 by the time it's paid for. Use the same idea in your negotiations. "Mr. Smith, by the time I pay you your $10,000, I'm going to have paid you over $30,000, and all that money will be yours because you'll be the bank."

Of course, using these techniques and being successful with them are matters of timing. Needs should be ascertained, fears assuaged, and a plan laid out and explained. All are necessary to piece the puzzle together.

CHAPTER *13*

LEVERAGING PEOPLE

One of the greatest advantages of investing in real estate is that there is so much good material written on the subject and so many good lecturers traveling the country to share their knowledge. I want to pose this advantage for your consideration because if you understand the reason behind this educational drive, you'll be able to use their knowledge to great benefit.

Obviously, there is not enough time or money to allow you to make all the mistakes mentioned in this book. Other people have preceded you who are more than willing to share their experiences with you, but this idea goes further than that. Wouldn't it be great if you could pick and choose what information you need to get into and out of deals, deals you've never thought possible? After all, why should you reinvent the wheel?

The investment methods of the different states are more similar than they are different. If a woman in Texas solved a problem that is similar to one that you're having, then why not study her method? Perhaps you'll use it all, or perhaps you'll only use part of it—or even improve on it.

One big advantage of having these experts available is that they are content to sell their books or charge a fee for their seminar and consulting—and that's it. You can take their ideas and put them to work in your area, and anything you make is your own.

Many times I've wished that I could get a commission on the growth and income others have created from reading my books and attending my seminars. I don't say this to brag (though a little of that is not bad because I'm proud of what my staff and I have done), but only to prove a point. There is no way to keep track of how much has been made with the Money Machine concept and the ideas from my other books.

I love it! It makes me feel good to have so many people taking charge of their lives and doing so much with so little. I don't really want a commission on any of it. People have worked for it, and now they can enjoy the fruits of their labors.

People ask me why I keep up this pace. This book is as good a forum as any to explain this. If you can understand my motives, then perhaps you will understand the motives of my fellow speakers, and this will motivate you to educate yourself further.

I've made a lot of money investing in real estate. I invested in real estate so that I could teach. I've worked toward that since I was seventeen years old. I wanted to go back to college and had to create an income source to do that. I turned to real estate to accomplish this.

About the time I was to start back to school, I was asked to write a book. *Real Estate Money Machine* was the result, and with that I was off on the lecture circuit. I now teach more than I ever could in college, and I teach people who really want to learn.

Their successes drive me on. I really enjoy taking people from a point of not understanding something to a point of understanding something and, additionally, to a point where they actually take the information and put it to work for themselves. I have dedicated my career to this end. All of my books and seminars have several constant themes: stay out of trouble, avoid clutter, create cash flow, and take control of all aspects of your investments.

Well, enough about me. What about the other authors and lecturers? I would say that very few of them are in it for the money. If that were the case, we'd follow our own investment advice and make more money by actually investing. Most are in it for the same reasons I mentioned. Most are good, honest people. You'll know when you hear them or when you read their books how much experience they've had and what kind of people they are.

I caution you, though, to beware. Test what they say for yourself. The story of the three little pigs is probably the best investment lesson ever taught. While two pigs were building their houses of straw and sticks, the third was building his house with bricks—one brick at a time. When the hard times came and the two other houses were lying on the ground, the brick house stood firm. Shouldn't our investment plan, our empire, be built the same way—one brick at a time?

Before I move on and explain how this can work for you, let me add one other thing. Most of these authors are extremely proud of their books, tapes, and other educational materials. Yes, there is a lot of outdated and irrelevant material out there, but there is also a lot of material with a great deal of thought and experience behind it. Look at how much pride they take in their books and seminars. The lecture circuit is a hard business. Very few make it. The only ones who do are honest and forthright and teach only good, functional information.

The Meaning for You

I'm sure that as you've read this you've thought of the books you've purchased and the money you've spent on seminars. Some of you might be thinking of gaining more education. Great! That's the way it should be. You'll open new doors, close a few bad ones, and polish the knobs on others.

It's a big investment world out there. We should stay educated. There is no standing still; the market isn't standing still, so neither should we. We should stay a step ahead by knowing what our education will do for us.

We're not going to invest in everything, but of those ideas we want to put to use, we can gather the best advice possible. Even contrasting opinions can help us establish a good function.

There are books and seminars on many different subjects. I don't recommend them all, but I've read and studied most of them. It's hard for me not to put in an advertisement here. My company publishes and sells many of these books, and we sponsor many seminars. But I do have a list of books and seminars I think are a must for different aspects of investing. I have included this list at the back of this book for your information.

Investment Groups

For the past several years many of the speakers have sponsored local investment groups. Almost every major city has at least one group that meets monthly. These people get together and have guest speakers talk about ideas pertinent to their area. Many have created buying privileges with local merchants. Anyone investing should attend because it's good to meet other investors and let them help you stay motivated. Call your local Chamber of Commerce for information on the group in your city.

Your Team

There is one lesson that I've had to learn over and over again. I bring it up here so that some of you won't have to make the same mistake. It sounds so simple, and in theory it is. But in real life it's a hard concept to institute and to keep working. We cannot do everything ourselves. We need a team of professionals.

When the poet John Donne wrote, "No man is an island," he stated a truth that we need to understand. This game of investments is for real. It is hard but exciting work. However, all of the excitement disappears when we make too many mistakes or when it turns to drudgery.

The need for a professional team is compounded in today's society when the complexities of investing demand specialization. Yes, we may be moving toward becoming a specialist, as I mentioned, but, in the meantime, we can use others not only to help us over the rough spots but to actually create opportunities for us.

There's no sense having people around who stifle everything we do. We need support. But it would be just as detrimental to have people around who will not throw a bucket of cold water on us occasionally. There must be a balance between the two. It's hard to find that balance and to keep it. So much enters into the picture besides truth; all kinds of feelings and personal biases become involved. My only advice is to keep cool. Consider the source and know what the source has to gain (or lose) by giving such advice.

Later on in this chapter, I'll list several possible members of your prospective team. I'll even show you ways to work with them, but before I do, let me list three points that will help put things in perspective.

First, the importance of having a team needs no long argument. I think we all know we need one. It may seem difficult, though, to find one—and it is. But I don't think that the process of setting one up or keeping it running should be so difficult that it stops us from doing the right thing.

As a matter of fact, this whole affair can really work to our advantage. There are many people who need help. What good professionals can do for us far outweighs the cost. They can get us into and out of properties we've never thought possible.

What I'm suggesting is that we look for and exploit the good that can happen. To explain this, let me tell of an experience I had with a professional roofer. Most of you probably want me to talk about real estate agents, lawyers, and CPAs. We'll get to that, but this story is too good and too pertinent to pass up.

I used a lot of inexperienced people to work on my properties. I found them at church or through friends or wherever. One Saturday I wanted to get a roof on a rather large house. I had had some experience with roofs before, so I thought it would take eight people to do the job.

Just before the work began, a professional roofer came by looking for work. He was very persuasive about his abilities. I really like a good sales pitch, so I took him on. This was new to me. The man actually wanted twice what I was paying any of the other eight workers. This man was so bold that I thought I'd have some fun, so I created a race. He would take one side of the house and the other eight workers would take the other side. He saw what I was doing and even went one better. He asked for the larger side.

They started work about 9:00 AM and dug in because the race was on. I checked in throughout the day, and after lunch it became clear who was going to win. The professional did win, but not by much. He finished his side at 3:30 PM, and the other eight finished at 4:00 PM His shingle lines were much straighter, and the whole side looked better. I became a believer. I paid the eight workers their $320 (8 people x 8 hours x $5 per hour = $320), and I paid the professional his $75 ($7^1/_2$ hours x $10 per hour) and threw in a $25 bonus so he'd come back and work for me again.

It doesn't take a mathematician to figure out which way was better. This episode taught me some valuable lessons. I am not suggesting that you don't use inexperienced people, only that you consider the alternatives. If I take on someone who needs training, I'll be patient, but if they don't move on quickly to becoming an expert, then it's time to reevaluate and get someone who doesn't need to be pampered.

I hope you will draw many lessons from this. The point I'm trying to make is that we can learn a lot from setting up our team. We can take this disadvantage and turn it into an advantage. It's how we look at it. Our attitude will affect a good or bad outcome.

Second, if your team is set up right, it will be with people who have a great deal of experience working with other people. Not all of their advice will be exactly right, but much of it will come from lessons they've learned from the mistakes of others.

I've mentioned that we can learn by listening to, watching, and reading about the mistakes of others. But now, learning from the mistakes of others through the eyes of our professionals adds a special dimension: we get commentary with advice.

Isn't it nice to see success and failure and understand the "why" behind it? This is trite, but it needs to be said: we can't make all of the mistakes ourselves. There's not enough time, energy, or money to make them all. These people have been around for a while. Call them anything you like, but you can lump them all together in one title called "professional problem solvers." The better they are with others, the better they will be with us.

Third, every one of us wants to be independent: independently wealthy and an independent thinker. We want to be self-made. Great! I don't want to take being self-made away from anybody. I do, however, want to help everyone achieve this by adding a thought or two about interdependence.

From the successful people I've known and read about, it seems that they knew where they stood with others. They also understood their relationship between things, events, and time. They became truly independent once they knew how to put these other forces to work for them.

The story has often been told of Henry Ford and his board of directors. Ford surrounded himself with the most talented, creative minds possible. When asked a question, he would turn to the members of his team and get their opinions. Once he had heard the various sides, he'd make a decision. This gave him the freedom to be himself. We all need that freedom. The better our team of professionals, the more independence we'll have.

Leverage

You probably think that I'm beating this subject to death. Maybe so, but please bear with me. It's a principle that just won't go away.

Remember before, when I mentioned leveraging our time, energy, and money? Now it's time to see if we can leverage people. Can we get a little to do a lot? The answer becomes readily apparent as we use an attorney to put the finishing touches on the purchase of eight duplexes. One time an escrow company fought through the assumption of two new loans. Another time the company helped us do the paperwork to close a four-plex that had caused so many problems. The cost was $420 (and that included title insurance).

Many of us spend a lot of time with our real estate agents. Agents only need one good investor, and they will become wealthy. Investors need only one good agent and they will become rich. Yes, it may take twenty to thirty hours of meetings and making offers for them to understand your plan before they can go on their own to represent you, but think of it, they could help you obtain fifteen or twenty properties this year—about one for every two hours of your time. Perhaps it won't be this simple, but it is conceivable. These professionals should only cost a fraction of the good they do for us.

Who Are They?

Obviously, the first person we need on our team is someone who can get us in and out of good deals. Good real estate agents will let us soar. They will find the properties, structure the offers, see it through to closing, and work out the bugs.

Yes, there may be a few agents out there who are less than efficient, but good ones are everywhere. Most are courteous and conscientious and will work out fine for you if _you_ follow through. Never give up on an agent. If you find one you like, make them work for you. Following through will make or break a real estate agent. There has been a real weeding out in the marketplace lately. I've seen the weak ones fall by the wayside. Most of the agents who are left are ready to go to work. Isn't it great that they can get paid so much? That may sound funny, but I've never seen a good agent get paid for someone else's work. They get paid by putting deals together. They bring people and ideas together and make things work. List your goals—the agents will make them happen. If you remember that you're the quarterback and they're the rest of the team, all will be well.

You may want to read the chapter called "My Real Estate Agent Loves Me" in _Cook's Book On Creative Real Estate._ We should make sure that everyone walks away happy. If you're serious about your investments, then find a serious agent to go to bat for you.

The next professionals we will need are law and tax consultants. My strongest advice here is that you do not use them for investment advice, which is not their area of expertise. Lawyers take care of legal aspects of the transaction such as transferring title, clearing encumbrances, and other technical matters. A CPA or other tax consultant can show you how a certain move will affect your tax situation, and perhaps help out with some book-keeping problems.

How do you find effective help? That's a tough question, and I wish I had an earth shaking answer. It's hard. The good ones are too busy, and, at that, most of them are not investors and therefore not up on what they need to know to solve our prob-lems. Questions like, "How much real estate do you own?" or "How much did you pay in taxes last year?" will help you eliminate people who do not practice what they preach.

The problem won't go away either. As soon as we find a good professional and the word spreads, then *they* get too busy to meet with you and keep up on the new changes. Keep trying, though.

The balance of the team is made up of escrow agents, title officers, and lending officers. You'll get to know them on a first name basis, and working with them will be fun as long as it remains in everyone's best interest to get the property closed.

Your team will also include your telephone, the local news-paper, and your library. Isn't it nice to have so many things at your fingertips to help you out?

Surround yourself with other investors. Meet with them, learn from them, get excited with them. It's amazing how clear things become when you take an experienced investor to lunch and then drop by a house you're thinking of buying. They've already leveraged their time, talent, and money, and you can copy or expand on what they've accomplished.

Summary
Those investors who get good at delegating are the most successful. But never delegate without a "return-and-report" system. Return and report puts into delegating the necessary guidelines to make delegating effective. For instance, I need a porch fixed. I have someone to do the work. The budget is $125

and I need it done by 3:00PM on Friday as I have tenants moving in this weekend. I will stop by between 11:00AM and noon that day to see how it is going. If something is wrong I want a report. I want to be educated and brought up to date so I can make adjustments. Don't ever assume that everything will get done. Make your team players check back in with progress updates. The only way to beat Murphy is to stay one step ahead of him. Ascertain problems, and cut them off at the pass. Set up systems to prevent things from going wrong.

Be specific with your check-back times and what you want accomplished by them. Treat your investment like a business and hold people accountable. One of the easiest ways to lose control is when people do not understand what they are supposed to do. Solve this by putting everything down in writing. You don't have time for misunderstandings.

I'm reminded of a woman who called her attorney. She wants a divorce. He asks, "Do you have any grounds?"

"Yes, we have a lovely acre."

"No, I mean do you have a grudge?"

"No, but we have a carport."

"That's not what I mean! Does he beat you up or something?"

"No, I get up before my husband every morning."

"Come on, lady, just tell me why you want a divorce."

"Because I just can't carry on a decent conversation with that man."

If you find yourself paddling upstream with people, then get everything down in writing so that there are no misunderstandings.

Once again, the problems created by setting up your team create great opportunities, opportunities to learn and grow and perhaps even to make a lot of money.

CHAPTER 14

OTHER INVESTMENT TIPS

While I was writing this book, I constantly thought of things that I wanted to write, but they didn't fit into any of the other chapters. A catch-all chapter was needed and here it is. These miscellaneous ideas are some of the most exciting and shouldn't be left out.

Lately I have had many clients come to see me because they were unhappy about the way they were being treated by their banks. One woman is a typical example. She had been dealing with one bank for over fifteen years and had gotten several short-term loans and a couple of long-term loans. Now, after she had taken an investment course, she went to the bank to get a loan in the same equity position and the same value position as the one she had recently paid off. The bank said no. The bank made it sound as if it was her fault that they would not lend her the money. Even though the bank admitted that some of their regulations had been changed, she felt bad because she didn't qualify under the new regulations.

The fact of the matter is that the banks didn't always have money to lend. If you want to avoid wasting time with banks, or savings and loans, that do not have the money either for second mortgages or even first mortgages, a good question to ask at the beginning of the initial interview is, "If I come in here with all the forms filled out and supply you with all the information you need and everything in my situation looks good for a loan, are you going to have the money to lend me?" This throws the ball into their court, and they're able to say, "No, we're not making loans at this time." Or they can say, "Yes, if you live up to this standard and these conditions, we will be able to make a loan of this amount of money."

Obviously, the next part of the questioning would be for determining what the interest rates are going to be and what the loan payback period is going to be, and the standards and conditions that the bank is going to make you live up to at that time.

But, in short, if the banks are feeling bad, they are going to try to transfer these bad feelings and make other people think that they are less than what they really are. Make sure that the banks stay in their place and you stay in yours.

Is It Easier To Get a Loan as an Employee or an Employer?

When employed people go to a bank for a loan, the information that they are able to supply the bank is readily verifiable. The fact that they are employed brings a certain amount of stability to their situation, especially if their employers are large or are well-known. The bank does not have to guess about the credit worthiness of the people.

If, on the other hand, the people who are trying to get a loan are self-employed and running their own businesses, the bank may be uncertain as to their reliability and it will require looking over books and records, possibly even auditing, rather than just verifying the standard employment record. The additional process is much more difficult and more expensive.

Women in Real Estate

Many of the letters I receive are from women. I'm very impressed with their abilities as investors. Three Kansas City schoolteachers, Carol Wilson, Linda Logan-Frank, and Jane Fowler, have put their thoughts into a book entitled *Wealthy Women: The Successful Woman's Guide to Real Estate Investing*. The following is an excerpt from their book. Granted, this excerpt is motivational in nature, but you'll feel their enthusiasm. I've sat with them discussing their properties. The book is an excellent "how to" book for people who think they can't make it.

> Real estate is fast becoming a great career for the woman who wants to work as well as the one who has to. The flexible hours are quite appealing for the working woman. It seems with the need for two incomes in a household this demand is making women more accessible.

> We have found that, for a woman, real estate investing is ideal. The reasons for this are many and varied. Just let us give you a few. Your experience as a wife, mother, and wage earner gives you just the background you need. All you have to do is add a few more hats to the many you already wear. Haven't you always handled being a cook, gardener, housekeeper, nurse, chauffeur, laundress, and so forth, as well as your primary roles of wife, mother, and wage earner? Well, all you have to do is add a few more hats such as shopper, negotiator, and manager, and your career can become exciting and your income unlimited. Women have always handled many responsibilities, and thus have learned to be organized. This is the prime requisite for a real estate career.

> Wouldn't it be nice to be free to go when your child's school called or to go to the grocery store in the middle of the day and avoid those crowds? Well, if you are your own boss, these are all possible, and any time saved can be spent on real estate.

> The amount of time you spend will determine what your income will be, and this is something that most women have not experienced.

> Certainly in our experience as teachers, if we worked very hard and spent long hours, no one offered to pay us more. Your income in real estate is your choice and hard work pays off!

Another advantage relating to money is the great tax savings that this career provides. Wouldn't your husband love to pay zero income tax? Well, this is certainly possible through your efforts. The money for the children's education, travel, or retirement can all be attained through real estate and wouldn't it be wonderful to have these responsibilities handled?

There are many advantages to this occupation—watching your financial statement grow, freeing up your time, and removing financial worries. But the greatest advantage for us has been the great variety of experiences, the excitement of new challenges, and the knowledge that our job need never be boring again, not even for one day!

People You Need On Your Team: as you begin to shop and buy, you will find that there are several people you need on your team.

The greatest asset to your "team" is a title company that knows you and that you trust. Our title company has answered many questions for us and saved us thousands of dollars in attorney costs. We always request to use our title company whenever possible. We feel free to ask questions when we need to.

From time to time you will need an attorney. Our first need for an attorney was when we were setting up our partnership. There are attorneys who specialize in real estate and they can be very helpful in drawing up a lease or evicting a tenant. Be sure to shop costs before you choose your attorney. Know how much you will be spending before you go to your attorney's office for a session.

As your number of properties increases you will be needing a group of repairmen on your team. We have a plumber whom we use regularly. He knows us when we call and promptly takes care of our problems. We use an electrician any time we have an electrical problem. We have agreed that we know nothing about electricity and we are too afraid to learn. Then you need a basic do-everything person who will do anything from hauling trash to trimming bushes.

We started out doing all of our own repairs and maintenance. As our number of properties began to grow we found that we were better off using our "brains" rather than our backs. We have decided that our time is better spent on shopping and buying a $15,000 equity. So gradually we have started using more and more repairmen on our team.

An aside: as Charles Schultz says, "People are much more resilient in the face of high interest rates than anyone thought."

The *Real Estate Connection* was a bimonthly real estate report. It was the nation's largest such service in terms of circulation, with articles, reports, tips, and strategies from various authors and investors.

This paper spoke with me about contracts and what they can do for the real estate investor. I feel that good contracts are one of the best kinds of investments a person can make. In the following interview, I explain in detail why contracts can be an investor's pot of gold at the end of the rainbow.

CONNECTION: Can you begin, Wade, by telling us exactly what you mean by the word *contract?*

COOK: When I talk about contracts, or contracts of sale, I'm talking about any form of owner-financing. That is to say that the owner of the property finances all or part of his equity instead of the bank.

CONNECTION: Is the word *contract* generally used around the country?

COOK: Yes, it is, but it could also be referred to as a mortgage, a deed of trust, or an all-inclusive trust deed.

CONNECTION: Are all of these different types of contracts, or are they just different names for the same thing?

COOK: In spite of the different names involved, there are really only two ways of using contracts. The first type of contract is when the seller takes his or her equity on installment payments and allows the buyer to assume underlying loans or mortgages. I'll illustrate this with an example: suppose that you still owe $36,000 on a house, but you sell the house for $56,000. You allow the buyer to assume your $36,000 loan and create a separate piece of paper for $20,000, which represents your equity and is secured against the property. The buyer agrees to pay you $200 a month at 10% interest until your equity is paid off (incidentally, this amortizes over an 18-year period). The paper you have created, regardless of what the document is called, is commonly referred to as a "contract," or as "paper."

The second type of contract is created when you wrap an already existing loan. That is to say that you, as the seller, maintain all underlying responsibilities and do not let your buyer assume any of the underlying loans. Instead, you create a new piece of paper on the total sale price. Your equity, then, is the difference between the receivable contract and the payable contract.

Let's use the previous example. This time, however, we maintain the existing loan for $36,000 and create a new contract for the total amount of $56,000. Let's say that the payment on the $36,000 loan going out every month is $360. Our receivable on the newly created contract is $620 per month. The net payment we receive every month, then, is the difference between those two figures, or $260 per month. This type of contract is the key to the Money Machine system. It doesn't take too many of these kinds of contracts to give us a nice, comfortable monthly living. And on top of that, there are no hassles with landlording or banks telling you who can and cannot buy your properties. You can also add to this the tax advantages of the installment sales method of claiming income.

CONNECTION: Once you have created a contract, what can you do with it?

COOK: There are a variety of things that can be done with contracts. The most obvious one is simply to hang on and live by the conditions of the agreement. You know that you will eventually be paid off, probably in one of two ways: either the contract will run the full distance or the purchaser will come up with the money to pay it off, either when someone buys the property from him, or perhaps when he decides to refinance.

The worst that could possibly happen (and it really isn't all that bad) is that you may have to foreclose on someone who doesn't pay as promised. In such an instance, you could either get the property back or have your loan taken over by the next person down the chain of tide. Remember, foreclosure laws vary greatly from state to state, so if this really were to happen, you should obtain good legal help.

Another possibility with contracts is to borrow against the equities. This is where you use your contracts as collateral with the banks. The banks will usually value the contract at about 50% of its face value. You then take this borrowed money (which is tax-free) and move on to bigger and better things. This same collateral use of contracts applies to dealing with individuals also. You might use this "paper" as collateral for security of performance. In such a case, you would get to use the contract as collateral, which means you would be able to give a seller some peace of mind as to your intentions to perform as agreed. And at the same time, you would continue to receive the payments from the contract itself. Not bad, huh? This is called "hypothecation" and is an effective tool.

CONNECTION: Can you use the paper you are holding to purchase other properties?

COOK: You bet! You can use it as a down payment for the face value of the contract. In all fairness though, the seller is getting a great deal in this case because he not only collects the full amount of the contract, but he'll also receive all of the interest income, which can be substantial. Take our example from before. If you wanted to use the $20,000 note for a down payment on a four-plex, let's say, then the seller would take the note and credit you for $20,000. In reality, however, the seller who took your note could easily reap $60,000 over the course of the note as a result of the interest involved. It's very unlikely that he will take the note at full value. The credit you will receive will probably be 50 to 70% of the face amount.

CONNECTION: What about selling your contract equities?

COOK: That is quite common in the investment world, so let's talk for a minute about what it is that those people who buy such contracts are looking for:

The first and probably the most important aspect that someone will be looking at is the yield. This tells them how fast they can plan on getting their money back. The yield, or rate of return on an investment, is identified by figuring the net cash received from the investment for a period of one year. You then figure what percent this amount is of the total amount paid out, invested. The percentage you come up with is the yield.

Let's go back to our example to see how it works. If someone purchased the $20,000 contract from us for $12,000 and was going to receive the $200 monthly payment, we would figure the yield (rate of return) by dividing $2,400 ($200 x 12 months) by $12,000 (what the buyer paid us for the contract). The answer would be 20%, meaning that the buyer of our contract received 20% of his money back in one year. Generally speaking, those who buy contracts are looking for at least a 20% yield and many times even more before they will even consider buying.

Then there are some other considerations, too, besides just the yield. The potential buyer of your contract will also consider the value of the property and more specifically the position the contract has in the value structure of the property. He will also want to know where the loan stands in the chain of title.

In all honesty, even if you decided to stay with a contract through the entire course of its amortized life, you probably wouldn't make it. As you can well imagine, most people get cashed out before too many years. Sometimes, someone is going to go to a financial institution for financing, which means that anybody holding any position at all on the property will get paid off. Even that shouldn't break your heart too much because, with that cash, you can still continue to grow.

CONNECTION: In your seminars, you talk about how contracts can help build a nice retirement situation for an investor. Could you talk about that for a moment?

COOK: Sure. You know, one of the really neat things about buying and selling contracts is that they not only provide cash flow for the present, but they can also provide income for the future.

When I get to be sixty-five or so, I don't want to be running around looking at houses and playing the whole game anymore. I want to be able to relax without any fuss or muss, and I want to be able to do it from a hammock in Tahiti if I want to. That's where the beauty of contracts comes in again. This time, however, instead of selling my contracts, I'm going to be the one who is buying them from other people. Just think of it. Now I will buy paper at fifty to sixty cents on the dollar and will collect monthly payments. Not only will I practically double my investment during the entire course of the payback, but I will also be the one who receives all the interest, too. And, of course, if that income becomes too substantial, I can always buy a few rentals and zero out my income through depreciation.

CONNECTION: When buying contracts, are there any more things to consider other than just the value of the property, the yield on your money, and the title status of the equity?

COOK: Yes, there are, and they include the following:

• Make sure that there is plenty of value above your loan. In other words, make sure that the value of the property is quite a bit greater than the amount receivable. This means that the people who are making your payments will have a lot to lose and therefore will have greater incentive to keep their payments current.

• Buy contracts that will cash out as part of the agreement, or on houses that will qualify for all types of financing later.

• Watch your repay percentage. Shoot for at least a 1% repay. This will make it easier to sell in case you need to later. This means a $30,000 note or contract has close to a $300 payment. The higher, the better.

• Make sure you have the right to resell your contract.

• Avoid contracts with all kinds of entanglements.

CONNECTION: Let's say that you have been running the Money Machine concept for a number of years and now you just want to slow down and buy a few contracts per month. Where should you start looking?

COOK: The most logical place to start buying con-
                   tracts with a discount is with your own
                   underlying loans. A lot of people that you
                   owe money to on contract would love to
                   have some cash, so buy your payables. By
                   doing so at a discount, you will decrease
                   your liabilities, which will help your debt-
                   to-asset ratio immensely. You also will
                   increase your net monthly income from
                   payments, get yourself closer to first posi-
                   tion on the property, and you will have
                   eliminated having to make one more
                   monthly payment.

CONNECTION: So which of your own contracts should you
                   buy first?

COOK: Look for the ones with high interest rates,
                   the ones with high payments in relation to
                   the mortgage amount, and the ones with
                   excessive restrictive clauses.

CONNECTION: Is there any more advice that you would like
                   to give our readers on buying contracts?

COOK: Whether you are on the payable or receiv-
                   able end, the contracts are good and have
                   tremendous advantages. Your only limita-
                   tion for using contracts is your imagination.
                   My advice to your readers is to further
                   educate themselves in this exciting area of
                   real estate and then get going!

Should You Get a Real Estate License?

The question of whether to be a real estate agent or not has
caused me much conflict in the past. I still find it hard to give
advice on this matter. It really is a personal choice, which only
you can make. Each way has its good points and its bad points.
Let me list some of these points here:

Good Points

1. You'll have access to most available properties. The more properties that you become familiar with, the better off you'll be when dealing with your own.

2. By sheer experience, you'll learn all the ins and outs of transferring property.

3. You'll be notified of training sessions and education (see Bad Points, item 1).

4. By dealing with other people, you'll learn from their mistakes, whether you're dealing with people or properties.

5. You'll come into contact with hundreds of people who may become potential investors/partners. These contacts will be valuable as your personal investments go through various stages.

6. You'll be able to associate with some really good people. Most agents are conscientious and hard working. The camaraderie developed within an agency has helped many agents to set goals, stay on track, and succeed.

7. When you do invest for your own portfolio, you'll save a lot of money on commissions.

8. If you had a license but were just being an investor, you would see many properties that you would not want to personally buy, but as an agent you could at least list them and pick up part of the commission.

9. Most agencies have sales incentives and achievement awards. Most people like to feel a part of these. They're fun and add to your feeling good about yourself. And when you feel this way, all of your relationships are better.

10. If and when you terminate being a full-time agent, you're ready to really roll. I've never met an agent yet

who thought that the time spent as an agent was a waste. If you work hard and smart, you're ready to think high and fly.

Bad Points

1. The training to be a good agent is necessary for success as an agent, but not all of this training is necessary to be a good investor.

2. The growth that you make investing can be severalfold higher than commissions earned.

3. The fact that you are an agent needs to be publicized when buying and selling. This may scare off people. It may also limit your rights when trying to get the best deal possible.

4. Most of an agent's growth is ordinary income and taxed at one hundred cents on the dollar. Most of an investor's growth is long-term and claimed at long-term rates (currently forty cents on the dollar). It must be noted that most good agents have good cash flows, though.

5. As an investor you can use many agents to work for you. This right still exists as an agent, but is curtailed by the fact that other agents may not want to work hard because you're an agent also and are entitled to part of their commission.

6. You will experience many time conflicts.

As you can see, this is no easy question. Personally, I avoided becoming an agent because I didn't want to play the agency game. I believed I could make more as an investor. Almost every time I made that decision (and I sat halfway through the state licensing classes three times), an agent friend would pick up several properties with just his commission as the down payment.

If I had it to do all over again, I think I would be an agent for a few years and profit from the ten good points to being an agent.

Then, when I felt I was ready, I would terminate it and just become a full-time investor. After all, owning and selling your own property is where the big money is.

Tips on Potential Fixer Uppers

Any investor who uses my Money Machine system knows that "fix-up" is a stage of the game where big dollars can be made—or lost. This section is designed to give you a few quick pointers on sizing up prospective investments.

First, you should remember that the idea is to turn houses. Generally, cosmetic work will take up the value of the house, but I have found that with some houses, the extra dollars spent trying to improve a place don't always take up the value that much more.

For example, a house in a run-down neighborhood has a top value on it—no matter how much money is put into it. So determine the top value of the house and fix it up only to reach that point. Any more fix-up is a waste of time and money.

It's always a good idea to see a property as soon after a good rain as possible. Water problems are obviously more likely to show up then. If you're from Seattle or Portland, this one will be easy. If you're from Tucson, use your imagination.

It's also a good idea to wear older clothes. If it's worth checking out, it's worth REALLY checking it out (of course, it is possible to overdo it)!

Take tools that might be useful when making your inspection— a penknife, flashlight, paper and pencil, plumb line, level or square, and perhaps even binoculars, if the property is several stories high.

Make notes as you go; you'll need them later when you estimate the costs of restoring the place.

Where do you start inspecting? Why not start at the top—the ROOF. Be sure to check tiles or shingles. Are any of them warped, cracked, or missing? If the roof is metal, paint should be in good condition. Make sure there is no moss growing.

Trouble you don't find on the roof, you may find in the attic. Do you see dark water stains on the underside of the roof or on rafters? If the attic isn't properly vented, you may see signs of mildew.

Next, you can check out the FOUNDATION and CELLAR. Cellars make checking foundations easier, but if there's just a crawl space, bite your lip and squirm your way under. Look for signs of movement in the foundation wall. Hairline cracks in the wall or along mortar joints usually aren't anything to worry about, but anything wider than a quarter of an inch may indicate serious problems.

Next, pull out your penknife to check the sill plate (that's the wooden piece atop the foundation walls that supports the wall above). Can you penetrate half an inch? If so, the house probably has moisture or insect damage. Check all other wooden parts of the house that are close to or in contact with the ground.

Crawl spaces should have at least one square foot of outside ventilation for every 300 square feet of ground. Ground should slope away from the house to prevent water from being trapped near the foundation.

From here, you might go to the OUTSIDE WALLS. Check upper parts of masonry walls for cracks and loose mortar. Loose or missing bricks, and soft, crumbling mortar invite water problems. Paint that is peeling, curling, or blistering can alert you to possible water problems as well.

Now to INSIDE THE HOUSE. You can inspect cracked plaster, which can usually be fixed without much difficulty. But if plaster feels spongy, it must be repaired and probably replaced. Especially note the plaster under bathrooms and at the ceiling— wall joints on the top floor. And about the FLOOR, some sag or tilt is to be expected, but make sure the cause is not structurally significant. If you don't know for yourself, you'd better ask someone who does.

Try to check MECHANICAL SYSTEMS—heating, plumbing, electrical—when they've been on for a while. Ask the owner for copies of fuel bills going back a year. Check the heating system—even if out of season. Look for black stains or rot on walls and floorboards around radiators. These can indicate that there may be leaks in the system.

Check the water pressure by flushing a toilet while the top floor tub and sink faucets are on. If the faucet water slows to a trickle, the piping may be clogged with scale or be otherwise inadequate.

A check of the ELECTRICAL SYSTEM begins at the fuse or panel box. If the box has cloth-covered wire or only three or four fuses, a complete rewiring is probably necessary both for safety reasons and for adequate power.

Many old houses have only one or two electric outlets per room. If you bought the house to do substantial remodeling, you may be required to bring this up to code, which usually means outlets every twelve feet or within six feet of any doorway.

Once you've made a complete inspection of the house, evaluate it. If it needs considerable fix-up and it doesn't look as if it will be worth the time and trouble, either talk the seller down to a price that will MAKE it worthwhile or forget it and go on to something else.

What About Interest Rates?

I did a little research and found out that making predictions is very hard. I put what I found in this book so you'll see that your guess is as good as mine. Shop around and learn what the rates will do in the short term, and that's about all you can do.

Talking about interest rates for the future is no easy task. As a matter of fact, making any kind of prediction for a month or even a week in the future concerning interest rates is quite difficult. The reason? It seems that those who should know what lies ahead aren't saying, and those who are predicting have no surefire way of knowing.

In an attempt to get some answers from people who should know the direction of our economic future, I assigned one of my staff members to contact those financial institutions that have the greatest effect upon the lives of individuals and investors alike. His assignment was to get any kind of interest rate forecast from these people. You would think that surely someone would be willing to tell the American people what they can expect within the next three to six months. So much for thinking.

When FHA/VA rates dropped to their lowest level in quite a while, it sent a lot of people to the bank in a hurry to apply for refinancing. With a downward trend in their interest rates, we thought that the FHA/VA people would be a good place to start. First call: the VA office in Washington, D.C.

The people at the VA refused to speculate about future mortgage rates. Instead, they gave a history of the previous year, ending with the pleasing story of the current mortgage rates. On to the FHA.

After being bounced around from person to person at the FHA (you might say it was a person-to-person call!), we finally got through to someone who dared say anything at all. He was just getting to the good part (his predictions), when someone else came on the line and interrupted the conversation. This strange new voice explained that no one there was allowed to speculate on the future of the mortgage rates. After that little interruption, we never did get to the good part of the other conversation. Before getting cool on the subject, however, our first contact there did give us some information. According to him, "the consensus is that the interest rate could come down a little bit more and bottom out at the end of the year." How much is a little bit? Well, the indication was that it could be by as much as a full point.

This consensus seems to be backed by some other sources as well. One reliable source in Washington said that regular home mortgages should be back down by the end of the year. This would be nice if, in fact, it does take place.

Chase Manhattan Bank, one of the nation's largest, was also tight-mouthed about the future. This, in and of itself, may confirm the fact that interest rates will continue to creep downward. After all, if they were to publicize the fact that rates would be coming down in the next three to six months, who, in their right mind, under normal circumstances, would borrow money right now?

I thought it was about time to go right to the horse's mouth, so I called the Federal Reserve Board. Now, a whole book could be devoted to this group, but I'll confine my statements to the information I was given. When they finally decided who it was that I should be talking to, I asked what it looked like in the next three to six months for interest rates. The woman I spoke to informed me that they did not know for certain, and even if they did know, they wouldn't tell. "Why?" I asked. "Because," she explained, "the Federal Reserve Board does not like to influence the market." Oh, brother . . .

So now I'll try my hand at it. We will probably see some stability in the current interest rates. The reason for this is very simple. If the powers that be want to stay in power, they need to stimulate the housing industry. To do so sets off a succession of events that must, out of necessity, take place.

To stimulate the housing industry, there must be actual sales of existing and new housing. To increase the number of sales, houses must be AFFORDABLE to people. Housing becomes more affordable for people when the monthly rates become reasonable and manageable again, and that means LOW MONTHLY PAYMENTS. How do the monthly payments get lower? By REDUCING THE INTEREST RATES, of course.

There is a pent-up demand for housing. There are literally thousands of people who want to buy their own homes but can't afford to. Sure, there are creative financing methods available, but to the general public, these techniques always carry a footnote. There are always scary terms attached. Although creative financing techniques work, there has not been enough time to educate people so that they feel comfortable and confident with such methods. All they know is the traditional way of financing a home, and unless the traditional mode of financing is available, there are many who will not buy. Low interest rates stimulate the housing industry and entice potential real estate buyers back into the market.

Interest Rate Summary

Combining all the information received about the future of interest rates for housing this year, we present the following summary:

1. Interest rates will follow the current trend and remain steady during the foreseeable future.

2. FHA/VA rates should drop hold at about 8% for a while.

3. Regular mortgage rates should hold at about 7¾%.

4. There is a good possibility that we may see 7% mortgage money again in an attempt to stimulate the housing industry.

All in all, it looks as though it will still be a good year for real estate investors.

A Brainchild Of Necessity

For a long time the documents used to buy and sell real estate were contracts (in all of their varieties) and mortgages. The document sweeping the country now is the AITD, or All-Inclusive Trust Deed. You say your state doesn't use deeds of trust. Maybe not, but read on.

Nothing changes in real estate unless there's a real need for it. Let me show you what happened with contracts and mortgages. I will write a short history of the evolution of and changes in the state laws and court cases that have effected this change. I'm not writing that this is applicable in all states, but it is cause for concern and action.

For many years the contract and mortgage have been in wide use. The contracts were used with all wraparound-type transactions. Then a seller foreclosed on a buyer for lack of payments under a contract and it was forced into court. Mortgages are "judicial foreclosures," which means that to foreclose, one must go before a judge. This whole process could take up to a year. Arising from this court case, contracts were also thrown onto the same ball field and deemed to be like mortgages, at least in foreclosure respects.

"Hold it!" said many attorneys all over the country: "We'll use a trust deed." You see, a trust deed has a "nonjudicial foreclosure." It takes two to four months and does not go before a judge.

Then a nail was driven into the mortgage/contract coffin (again, in many states) that really made them inappropriate. Once foreclosed on, people could come back and sue for their equity. Now, most people don't know this, so they just walk away. Even if they sue, the amount of equity would have to be substantial and damages proven, but nevertheless more doubt was placed on these old forms.

The trust deed came to the rescue again: no equity rights ("equitable provisions"). You could get the house back and get on with it.

To continue the history—we became creative with our real estate transactions, and we needed a wraparound trust deed. Thus, the AITD. The words *all-inclusive* mean wraparound. Now we can take a down payment and finance the balance in a wraparound manner with all of our foreclosure rights intact.

These rights should be the first to be looked at when it comes to documentation and agreements. Keep pushing for deeds of trust in your state. But remember, state law takes precedence over legal documents. It's a long, hard process to get lawyers, title companies, and legislation to change—but it is well worth the effort.

You see, you need documents that allow you to correct any mistakes in judgment you've made. We all need to place more emphasis on making correctable decisions than on making correct decisions.

A Caution On Adjustable Rate Mortgages

Adjustable rate mortgages are fast becoming the act to follow in the area of conventional financing. This type of mortgage was especially popular among first-time home buyers in 1983. Did these first-time home buyers bite off more than they will be able to chew? Let's go back to the beginning for just a moment.

In the 70s and 80s lending institutions, especially thrifts and loans, were burned a bit by being locked into low-yielding, long-term mortgages, while interest rates rose.

The Adjustable Rate Mortgage (ARM) was emphasized by the thrifts to avoid a recurrence of the crisis situation in which they had found themselves. The adjustable rate mortgage can be revised upward if the cost of money to the lending institution rises. By 1984, 65% of all mortgages made by thrift institutions were adjustable, according to the U.S. League of Savings Institutions. That's about double the proportion of the year before.

One big reason for the sudden upsurge is probably the fact that lenders are offering very attractive introductory rates for the first year of a new mortgage. Those rates are sometimes three full percentage points lower than the rate offered for a fixed rate mortgage.

After the first year, however, adjustable rates can be changed up or down in accordance with a specified index, such as the treasury bill or other money market rates. There is usually a maximum amount of change, frequently two percentage points, and an overall cap beyond which the rate cannot be raised.

The result of all this is that many potential home buyers can now qualify for mortgages they previously wouldn't have been able to get or carry. There is a potential catch. If the incomes of the new home buyers do not rise sufficiently to enable them to pay increased mortgage costs in the years ahead, they could be forced into default.

If you are considering the option that an adjustable rate mortgage offers, you should ask your lender these questions:

- How often is the rate adjusted?

- How often is the payment rate adjusted?

- What is the spread above the index?

- Is there a cap on the base rate? A bottom limit?

- Is that cap over the entire term of the loan or just for any consecutive number of years?

- May I have a five-year history of the index you are using?

- Where is that index published?

It's very important that you know the direction in which your index is moving so that you can decide early whether to seek fixed rate financing even at a somewhat higher cost—to avoid a big hike in your payments after the first year.

Do your homework well on this one. You could save yourself a lot of lost sleep in the future.

Advice on Financial Statements

Your financial statement should sing your song well. This will not be a lengthy discourse on how to set one up, but a discussion on a few techniques that I've learned over the years that have helped immensely to portray my financial statement in a better light.

First of all, it is common practice to list all the assets on one page and all the liabilities on another page. As you may know, in real estate this can be very complicated. While the assets are producing income and the liabilities are producing debt service, sometimes the liabilities page could be quite extensive in that the assets page shows a rental with so much income, and on the liabilities page it may list four or five loans with money going out. The large amount of small loans taking up the liabilities page space may be overwhelming to the banker or to anyone looking at your statement.

After having several financial statements prepared professionally by one of the best CPA firms in town, I went to them and

179

said that I'd like to change the format of the financial statement. We discussed it at length and came to a determination that on the same page we could list the properties that were rental properties, by address, estimated market value, gross rents, liabilities in terms of monthly payments and expense, the last column showing the net profit the rental was producing.

Another page would deal with nothing but real estate contracts. It would list the receivable contract/contracts or notes. Then it would list payable contracts or notes. And, again, the last column would list the net monthly cash flow.

Another section of the financial statement would list the properties that were being held pending resale. This page would not include the monthly payments.

Now bankers could look on one page and see the amount of assets and liabilities of all properties, but most of all, they could see the amount of the net monthly payment. They could see that especially in the contract area, and hopefully in the rental area, there was a good, positive cash flow, and that these assets did not only represent equities, but that they also spun off income. The bankers were able to read this in an easy-to-understand format.

Banks are hard to work with. The next section gives a clue on what can be done.

Sweeten the Pot

Many times, in trying to get financing, there needs to be a kicker, some catalyst thrown in that will make the deal come together.

Once I had the opportunity of buying five houses. Up to this time, Harry (my banker) had been making loans to me and had watched intently as I built up my net worth. I could tell by his questions that he was thinking about getting into investing himself. And, sure enough, in a few months, he even asked me where he could find a good deal. He wanted my opinion about some ads in the newspaper that he had seen.

About that time, I came across five properties that were really in a run-down condition. I needed to get $10,000, but Harry's bank had just put clamps on making loans. I had only been with the bank for six months at the time, and they were lending money only to old customers who wanted to get $50,000-plus loans. I needed this $10,000 for the repairs on these properties, and I probably couldn't proceed without the loan. While I was talking to him, I said, "Look, Harry, you're looking to get into some properties now. How about it if I sell these properties to you at 10% below the fair market value when they're all fixed up?" He immediately asked me what I meant, and I laid out the whole plan.

The kicker was that he was lending the bank's money, but I was agreeing to sell the properties to him personally. After hearing the deal, he realized how good it would be for him. He processed the loan, getting it through his loan committee in three days.

Each one of these properties was in such a run-down condition that it was selling for 50% of its market value—possibly even 40%. One, worth $40,000, was selling for $18,000. One, worth about $35,000, was selling for $20,000. One, worth about $45,000, was selling for $20,000. And it was a whole package deal, where I could buy these properties for nothing down.

The large amount of fix-up that was needed was actually $15,000, and I needed the bank's $10,000 to have enough. The deal was that at the end of the time, when all of the houses were fixed up, I would sell them to him—the $40,000 house for $36,000 with a 10% down payment and the $45,000 house for $40,500 with $4,050 down.

He had saved about $20,000 but only had about $15,000 that he wanted to tie up in properties. It just so happened that the eventual down payments on the five properties were going to come to about $15,000. He was very excited about this because he knew that 10% financing was a good deal for him and that this amount would be more than the $10,000 that the bank was going to be lending out. His neck as a loan officer was not going to be sticking out, and he was going to be able to not only put a loan together but end up buying these properties as well.

Just about the time he was about to say "yes" and start processing the loan papers, he rocked back in his chair and said, "How much is this really worth to you?" I thought, "Oh no, he's going to ask for some more off, or he's going to want something else." But all he said was that he knew nothing about tenants and that he would like to buy each property already rented. I agreed in writing that as soon as the properties were fixed up and ready to go, I would get signs up and get them rented, or I would help him even after he bought them. My crew and property manager would be at his disposal to help him get the properties rented.

You never know what makes people tick. Keep fishing for possible solutions. Persistence in negotiating has turned many a hard deal around.

Closing Costs

Closing costs can really drag you down. There are so many unexpected things that can happen. Many people have written asking me questions. I'll use some of theirs and mine in this section in a question-and-answer format. Remember, saving even a few hundred dollars on each deal can really add up.

QUESTION: I'm buying a home, and like most home buyers, I cannot afford to pay the full purchase price in cash. I have enough for the required down payment and intend to apply to a lender for a loan for the balance. Is that all the money I'll need?

ANSWER: Not quite. When you apply for a loan, you'll discover additional home-buying expenses associated with settlement.

QUESTION: What is settlement?

ANSWER: Settlement, sometimes called "closing," is the transfer of ownership of a home from the seller to the buyer. Greatly simplified, these are the steps that lead to final purchase:

• You and the seller sign a purchase agreement or sales contract. Usually, at this point, you are asked to make an initial payment, often called an "earnest money deposit," as evidence of your intention to buy the property.

• Then you apply to a financial institution or other lenders for a loan. It's a good idea to have a clause in the purchase agreement that makes your obligation to buy contingent on your ability to arrange the financing. Otherwise, you might lose any initial payment you've made if the lender turns you down.

• The sales agreement you've signed describes the property, states the purchase price, sets forth the method of payment, and usually names the date and place where the settlement or actual transfer of the property will occur. This meeting, or transaction, is sometimes called the "closing," or the "passing of papers."

• A new deed will be prepared, transferring ownership of the property to you. Your lender will require your signature on a document, usually a promissory note, as evidence that you are personally responsible for repaying the loan. Also, you will sign a mortgage on the property as security to the lender for the loan. The mortgage gives the lender the right to have the property sold if you fail to make the payments. Sometimes a deed of trust or security deed is used instead of a mortgage, but the legal effect is virtually the same. Before you exchange these papers, the property may be surveyed, appraised, and inspected for termites or other structural problems, and the ownership of the title will be checked in county and court records.

• The last step is the settlement, generally a meeting between buyer and seller. The meeting may include representatives of the lender, title company, real estate broker, and any lawyers hired by either party. You, as the buyer, must bring money enough to complete the sale, and the seller will transfer the property to you. In some sections of the country, however, there is no formal meeting of buyer and seller. The transaction is handled by a third party known as an escrow agent.

QUESTION: This all sounds very complicated. How can I find out what fees will be charged to me?

ANSWER: Within three days of written loan application, the Real Estate Settlement Procedures Act (RESPA) requires that you receive a *Special Information Booklet* and a Good Faith Estimate of settlement charges from the lender. At settlement, or shortly afterward, you will receive a Uniform Settlement Statement, or HUD-1 form, required by RESPA, which is your permanent record of all the final settlement charges. You are entitled to review the settlement statement one business day before settlement.

QUESTION: What is RESPA?

ANSWER: The objective of the Real Estate Settlement Procedures Act (RESPA) is to reduce consumer settlement or closing costs. The act applies to federally related mortgage loans. While almost all home loans fall within this category, there are a few exceptions, such as assumptions and refinancing. Under the provisions of the act:

- Lenders are required to provide loan applicants with a *Special Information Booklet* and a Good Faith Estimate of settlement costs at the time of application.

- Persons conducting settlements are required to provide buyers and sellers with HUD-prescribed settlement statement (Form HUD-1).

- Borrowers have the right to review the HUD-1 form one business day before the closing.

- Payment or receipt of unearned fees or kickbacks is prohibited for referrals connected with settlement services.

- Sellers are barred from requiring that the buyer purchase title insurance from a particular company.

- The amount the lender can require a borrower to deposit in an escrow account is limited.

QUESTION: What are settlement costs?

ANSWER: Settlement costs, sometimes called "closing costs," are all the charges and fees associated with transferring ownership of your new home to you, processing the loan papers required before your lender will forward to the seller the money being provided to help you buy your home, and taking the steps necessary to assure that your lender will have a valid claim against your property for the repayment of your home-purchase loan. Other costs that must be paid at settlement are the adjustments to be made between you and your seller for certain yearly payments, referred to as "prepaid items," for which you may be charged on a pro rata basis.

QUESTION: Could you be more specific about these items? I'd like to know exactly what I'm paying for.

ANSWER: Depending on where you live, these are some of the charges you may be required to pay:

• Initial service or origination fee. This is the lender's fee for originating the loan. In most areas lenders charge 1% of the face value of the mortgage. In transactions for existing structures involving FHA and VA, the origination fee can be no more than 1% of the mortgage amount. Keep in mind that the fee is in addition to the charges listed below, and may be subject to negotiation.

• Points. Lenders often find that mortgage loans are not as profitable as other forms of investments. They, therefore, charge an additional fee, called a "point," or a "loan discount." Each point is equal to 1% of the amount of the loan and the money is collected at closing. In FHA and VA transactions, the home buyer is not permitted to pay points. No limit, however, is placed on the number of points that may be paid by the seller.

• Appraisal fee. The lender often requests an appraisal of the property. In the case of a HUD-insured or VA-guaranteed mortgage loan, the fee is established by government regulations.

• Recording fee. The local government may charge a fee for recording documents pertaining to the sale.

• Credit report. The buyer's credit history is usually required by the lender before making a loan.

• Termite inspection. Many lenders request that the property be checked for harmful pests before granting a loan.

• Survey. The lender may require a survey to determine the precise location of the house and the property.

• Title search. A title or abstract company or a lawyer will search through records of previous ownership and sale to establish the right of the seller to sell the property to you.

• Title insurance. The mortgagee's policy protects the lender's interest in the property against any title defects not disclosed by the title search. Only one premium payment is required, and it is due when the insurance policy is issued. This policy does not cover your interest. *If you want protection for yourself, you must obtain an owner's policy.* Whether the buyer or seller pays for one or both of these policies varies with local custom.

• Attorney's fees. In addition to any fees for your own attorney, you may be required to pay for the legal services provided to the lender in connection with your loan.

• Preparation of documents. The deed, mortgage, and other papers necessary to complete the sale must be prepared by a lawyer, the lender, or some other party.

• Settlement fee. A charge may be made for handling the settlement transaction.

• Mortgage insurance premiums. This insurance is often required if the loan will exceed 80% of the property's value or if it is insured by the Federal Housing Administration (FHA). The fee is paid to a company or government agency, which guarantees the lender against loss if you fail to make your payments. This kind of policy should not be confused with mortgage life or disability insurance policies designed to pay off your mortgage in your behalf in the event of your physical disability or death.

• State or local transfer taxes. In some localities, these taxes are levied when property changes hands or when a real estate loan is made.

• Reserve accounts. The lender may require that accounts be set up to pay bills for taxes, assessments, property insurance, or mortgage insurance premiums that fall due in the future. These may be called "reserve," "escrow," or "impound" accounts (this must be done if the loan is FHA-insured). You will pay one twelfth of the annual amount of these bills each month with your regular mortgage payment. When the bills fall due, they are paid by the lender from the special account. At settlement, it may be necessary to pay enough into the account to cover these amounts for several months so that funds will be available to pay the bills as they fall due.

• Adjustment of prepaid items such as real estate taxes and municipal service charges. Prepaid items involve the charges levied against a property on a yearly basis. Suppose the builder or seller has paid the entire year's taxes on the house, but sells before the year is over. Either is entitled to a refund from the buyer for the portion of the year that the buyer will own the house. This also is true for special assessments, such as those for street or sewer improvements, and for property insurance if an existing policy is being transferred to the new owner.

• Escrow fee. In some areas, a third party handles the entire settlement without the presence of the buyer or seller or other parties to the transaction. This person is called an "escrow agent," and a fee is charged for these services.

• Miscellaneous. Notary fees, inspection fees, charges for photographs of the property, a schedule of mortgage payments, real estate commission, and other incidental expenses payable by either the buyer or seller may appear on the statement.

QUESTION: Should I hire a lawyer to help me?

ANSWER: It's a good idea, particularly if the sale is complicated or if you are not sure you completely understand the terms of the sale. Remember, any lawyer not involved at your request is representing the lender, seller, or someone else and is not responsible solely or primarily for protecting your interests. If you do hire a lawyer, choose someone who is familiar with real estate law in the area where the property is located so that you have the benefit of the best possible advice. Hire your attorney early enough to review the terms of the purchase agreement before you sign it.

QUESTION: If I am required by the lender to pay for title insurance, can I be sure it will protect me?

ANSWER: Since there are two kinds of title insurance, you should not assume you are protected. *A lender's* or mortgagee's title insurance policy protects only the lending institution up to the amount of the outstanding loan. Even though most lenders require the buyer to pay the premium, that does *not* mean that the buyer's interests will be protected. An *owner's* policy is necessary to protect the owner against loss. If the lender does not require a lender's policy, the owner's policy may be purchased separately. It is usually much less expensive if purchased simultaneously with a lender's policy at the time of settlement.

QUESTION: If a lawyer searches the title to the house I'm buying, will I need an owner's title insurance policy too?

ANSWER: You must make that decision. Ordinarily, when a lawyer searches a title, only public records are examined. In most cases, this procedure will uncover problems with the title. However, some types of land title problems, such as a past deed that was forged or signed by a minor, will not appear on the public record. And you could not expect to learn of such problems no matter how carefully a lawyer searched the public records. Title insurance protects you against these and other risks, and also pays the expenses of going to court if it becomes necessary to establish the validity of the title.

QUESTION: Are different types of policies available?

ANSWER: In some states, the policy forms and rates are set uniformly by law. In other states, both rates and policy coverage may vary from one company to another. You should question the title company or lawyer closely to be sure you are getting maximum protection at minimum cost.

QUESTION: Home-sale advertisements of some developers say, "No closing costs; just prepaid items." What are they talking about?

ANSWER: The claim of no closing costs means that the developer is absorbing the costs, but often the costs have been passed on to you anyway in the total price of the property. You'll be paying interest on them, as part of the loan balance, with every mortgage payment. If you have sufficient cash, you might consider paying them when you close the sale and avoid the additional interest. Many developers have put together package deals wherein they are able to obtain the above services at a lower cost than would be the case if each were obtained separately.

QUESTION: Are all of these fees necessary?

ANSWER: Many of these services are required by state or federal law. They include the property tax adjustments, transfer taxes and recording fees, low down-payment loans, and the mortgage insurance premium. Lenders are usually required by law to have an appraisal, a credit report, and title search for each loan they make. However, the law does not generally require title insurance or a survey, and whether these are required is up to the lender. Some lenders do not impose an initial service fee or other miscellaneous charges, some handle the preparation of most documents and the settlement itself without charge, and others require the parties to the transaction to pay for these items. In these respects, lender practices vary greatly.

QUESTION: Are there any steps I can take to reduce the closing costs I have to pay?

ANSWER: You can shop for services, negotiate fees, and ask questions. Here is a checklist of actions you should consider:

• Before signing a sales contract, negotiate with the seller to share with you the cost of such items as the settlement or escrow fee, points, title insurance, survey, and transfer taxes.

• If a survey is required, commit the seller to give you the old survey and an affidavit that no changes have been made in the structures on the property that would overlap the boundaries. Many lenders will accept this in lieu of a new survey.

• Find out which title insurance company wrote the policy the seller bought when purchasing the house. Contact that company and ask for a lower rate (sometimes called a "reissue rate") on your title insurance. Most companies will reduce their charges if not too much time has elapsed since they last searched the title.

• Insist on the right to choose your own lawyer, title company, surveyor, or other necessary suppliers of settlement services. Don't be afraid to shop around and to bargain with suppliers of settlement services. These include the lawyer, title company, escrow or settlement company, lender, and surveyor. Be sure the fees they quote are totals, with no extra or miscellaneous charges to be added.

• If you hire a lawyer, make it clear that you and only you are the client. Ask whether the lawyer is receiving a rebate or commission from the title company or any other party, and, if so, that it be refunded to you.

• Read the *Special Information Booklet* you receive when you apply for a loan. Then study your Good Faith Estimate carefully. Request an explanation of any items you don't understand or feel are excessive.

Remember that you have a right to review the settlement statement *one* business day before settlement so that you can estimate how much money you will need to bring with you.

CHAPTER 15

IDEAS THAT WORK TODAY

Towards the end of the decade is an interesting time to stop and take a look back at the predictions made as we moved into the new decade. Did all of the predictions come true? Did any of them come true? And no matter how we are headed as a nation, where are we headed as individuals? I bring up this point because in every phase of the economy, from the depths of the Great Depression to the prosperity of the 1980s and 1990s a handful of people have made their fortunes while the rest of the world waited for "the right time."

Now is the right time. Your own financial dream is your call to arms. Nobody can do it for you. There are experts waiting to help you, but you're the one who has to take the bull by the horns and make something happen.

In the 1950s it was location, location, location; then in the 1970s it was terms, terms, terms; today it's cash flow, cash flow, cash flow. This sentence is a great lead-in for us to explore the changes in real estate investing. Most of the books on the market today about investing were written in the 1970s and 1980s. Those books were great for those times, but we all know that times have changed. If you are reading the older books, it is my contention that you should do most things mentioned in these books backward. That's how much the investing environment has changed. So what do we do now? What are our guidelines for today?

In order to make your real estate do for you what you want it to do, you've got to know how each property is going to fit into your plan, and you need to make it work for you. Your primary concern is to forget about the tax benefits as a primary reason for investing in a property. That's an after-effect. It's nice to have, but you've got to go for value. If you're investing in a limited partnership, or in any kind of investment, you must look for the diamonds in the rough.

The following eleven points are a guide to investing now, but I hope you'll see how each one can be used at any time and in any phase of national feast or famine.

A Balanced Portfolio

First, create a balanced portfolio: in my seminars I often ask how many of the attendees would like to have a tax problem. Most people *would* like to have a tax problem. Many of you reading this book do not have a tax problem. If you start investing for cash flow, you will create a tax problem.

At the beginning, you buy properties specifically to build up cash flow. Then you say, "Well, I've got enough of that, now I've got to move on and start buying a few properties and holding them for the tax write-offs." This is called "creating a balanced portfolio." You begin to realize that cash flow, tax write-offs, and growth for the future don't happen one, two, three. They happen together. You can get started with cash flow, but very quickly you've got to start the other aspects going. Wouldn't it be awful to have created your monthly income and, instead of keeping it all, you had to give half of it to the IRS?

Investing in real estate solves problems. To invest effectively, we need to understand exactly what problems we have that real estate can solve. It would be a waste of time to just buy properties without understanding what we want the properties to do for us. A good investment should fit our own situation like a piece in a jigsaw puzzle.

Let's discuss some aspects of the three reasons for investing in real estate. The first reason is cash flow. Cash flow can be developed in a number of ways. One way is through rental income, which is still a good way, but which is not as effective today as it was in the 1960s and 1970s. Cash flow can also be generated by the creation of notes, or by buying and selling property and receiving the cash. Everyone needs more cash flow.

The second reason is tax write-offs. Tax write-offs come about as a result of the tremendous leverage possible in real estate, and the federal government's lenient treatment of the leveraged growth. A $100,000 property will give approximately a $9,000 tax write-off. If we're able to buy that $100,000 property with only $5,000 down, that is almost a 2-to-1 write-off.

The third reason, growth, is the basis for seven out of every ten fortunes made in the United States. Growth can be a slow buildup of equity in a few properties held for many years, or, in a more short-term way, by buying and selling quickly and using the profit to buy even more properties, pyramiding equities into real wealth. This is the theme of my first book, *Real Estate Money Machine*, and most of my lectures.

Most real estate advisors push one of the three advantages almost to the exclusion of the other two, but investors need to strike a balance between the three. Every purchase can provide all three benefits; you should concentrate on the benefit you need most, but do not neglect the other two.

When you are beginning your career as an investor, you need a steady monthly income to free you from the forty-hour-a-week grind. That's easily done by buying, fixing up, and selling a property quickly—selling it and creating a note that will pay $100 a month for twenty years or so. That is the basis of my Money Machine concept. Enough notes and you will not have to depend on a job to pay the bills.

The crazy thing is that as I speak at conventions across the country, people who have never bought one property can't wait to begin investing for the tremendous tax benefits they've heard about. I don't understand that—they don't have a tax problem, and they're looking for a solution. Once they have a healthy monthly income built up, then they should buy all the tax write-offs they can get.

For the person making $50,000 or more a year, tax benefits are a must. These people don't need a lot more monthly income, but they do need to keep Uncle Sam at bay every April. A person living at this income level should, of course, buy tax write-offs, but not to the exclusion of equity growth. The properties that provide long-term growth will leave the upper-middle-class in the upper-middle-class even after retirement.

Besides the advantage of offering all three benefits, real estate may be paid for over a long period of time. If you buy $100,000 worth of real estate, you have the next thirty years to dig up the money, and you can buy the property with as little as 2 or 5% down. Then the tenants pay off the loan. Only real estate pays for itself.

If you were to go to an estate-planning seminar and they were talking about the stages every successful investor goes through, you would find that most people follow the same basic pattern. In the first stage, they accumulate assets and build up income. It is the time for muscle work, or wise leveraging—but hard work, nevertheless. Unfortunately, too many people stay in that stage all of their working lives and have nothing to look forward to when the time comes to retire.

The second stage, reached by a small percentage of the population, comes after assets have been built up to the point where they can be invested. Again at this stage, several of the players are wiped out of the game, as they watch their chips move to the IRS side of the table, or lose their investment money through neglect and mismanagement.

For those who have been prudent enough to recognize all three stages and who have put their assets to good use, the third stage of investing is the kind of retirement that the other 95% of the population dreams about.

Real estate investing can take you through every stage. Whether you call it cash flow, tax write-offs, or growth—or accumulation, maintenance, or retirement—it means that you can look forward to a good end product.

Success is a product of initiative, persistence, and foresight. Real fortunes are created; and the overwhelming majority of these fortunes have been created by people who have invested in real estate. These people—most of whom started with little or nothing—became multimillionaires not only by investing in real estate but by staying in balance.

Imagine investing strictly for cash flow—for a monthly income—by buying and selling quickly, creating a note each time. Many of you know from attending my Money Machine seminars that I really get excited about buying a property, fixing it up, and selling it, taking a note for my profit, but building cash flow will bring the IRS down on you quickly. You need to shield that income *and* you need to keep a few properties for future growth, getting ready for retirement.

The best real estate investments will pay for themselves, give you cash flow, shield your income from the IRS, *and* build up growth for the future. If you are not actively investing now, learn how and begin creating your own wealth now, and stay in balance.

Develop A Team

Second, develop a team: nobody has enough time to make all the mistakes. I know that sounds like a cliche, but if you're serious about succeeding as an investor, you simply do not have the time to learn everything the hard way.

You should surround yourself with people who have studied and have experience with every step of buying, fixing up, managing, and selling property. It is one of the most frustrating experiences in the world to be ambitious and aggressive and to get out and buy properties, and then not have a team to help you solve the problems that are created by owning too much property, such as making a lot of money.

One interesting thing that I have been doing recently in my seminars is to ask how many people are afraid to buy their first property. A lot of hands go up. Then I ask those who have purchased five or more properties to raise their hands, and almost the same number of hands go up. I ask them to keep their hands up for a moment, while I ask another question. I say, "If one of the newer investors in this room was willing to take you out and buy you a nice lunch, how many of you would go with them to look at a house or two in the afternoon?" Almost all of the hands stay up. I then ask, "Who learns more in a teacher/student situation?" Invariably the people—especially those who have been teachers—agree that the teacher learns more.

We all need a bucket of cold water thrown on us once in a while to remind us that we need to have professionals (attorneys, CPAs, and others) available to lend their expertise to our careers as investors.

Here is a hint when looking for professionals: a good question to ask is how much they paid in taxes last year. If they are paying a lot in taxes, they obviously are not investing in real estate, and if they aren't investing, they probably aren't interested, and they aren't keeping abreast of the latest laws. You should look for people who are actively investing when you put together a team of experts.

One further note here: Peter Drucker, in *The Effective Executive,* said that we should base our opinions on a foundation of conflicting opinions. If you have a team, including a spouse, friends, other investors, and professionals, and they all agree with you on every investment, you aren't getting the constructive criticism you need. It's time to back off and say, "Wait just a minute now. Please tell me all the negative things you can think of about this investment." Agreed, it's hard to go through life with negative people looking over your shoulder and criticizing your every move, but you should have a good base of conflicting opinions in order to help you make a sound decision.

Buy Value

Third, buy value: too often, I see people buying real estate to solve one problem when the whole picture should be taken into consideration. For instance, I recently heard about a man who bought a four-plex for $85,000, did a little fixing up, and then, by asking for little or no down payment, he was able to sell it for $120,000. People were happy to pay the higher price (despite the fact that the four-plex was worth $95,000 to $100,000) because they could get tax write-offs on the whole $120,000. It may have a great tax write-off, but it was a bad investment in all other respects. We buy real estate so we can sell it in the future, or create notes or cash. The tax write-offs should be the icing on the cake. We should buy value—properties that have strong investment qualities, such as a good purchase price and high marketability when it comes time to sell.

The point I make in my seminars is that our first consideration when we buy should be the investment quality. When we sell, our first consideration should be the tax implication.

Value is *dollar value*. For instance, if you can buy a property with a real market value of $120,000 for $100,000, you are buying instant equity-dollar value. You will have the tax write offs on the full $100,000, but even better, you have dollar value that you can sell or trade to buy more property and create even more value.

If, on the other hand, you buy the property that is actually worth $100,000 for $120,000, you will have to hold onto it for the next two or three years (at least) and wait for the real value to catch up to the purchase price. Which investment is better?

Buy value. Value in terms of dollar price, marketability, and rentability. If you concentrate on investing for value, all of the other benefits will fall into line.

Stay Educated

Fourth, stay educated: progress is based on continued education. Every advance that mankind has made has been a result of combining past knowledge with new ideas. We will solve the problems of tomorrow with the information we've garnered today.

When Derik Bok, Dean of the Harvard Law School, said "If you think education is expensive, try ignorance," he said a mouthful. The cost of education is a thousand times cheaper than the cost of ignorance. As investors, we need a constant supply of new ideas and information. We should educate ourselves on a daily basis by talking to people, reading books, listening to tapes that will keep us constantly fresh, being constantly alert to new ideas.

It is easy to stay educated in real estate because there are so many great investors who have turned educators. For the love of education, they have developed books and tapes. You are able now to turn your car into a "university on wheels," as Denis Waitley, a well-known educator in the field of achievement and motivation, says. Imagine having some of the most experienced, professional investors sitting next to you in your car, as you drive to work, giving you a personal lecture and answering your questions. Everything they say may not apply to you, but you should be able to get at least one good idea with every tape, one motivational idea to keep you going and help you persist a little bit longer.

It would be unfair for people to teach seminars and to get other people excited about investing, and then not have books and tapes available for them so they can take resource materials home.

People often come up to me after buying my set of books and tapes at a seminar or convention and ask, "Now what do I do?" And I reply, "Read a couple of chapters and then go buy a property. Start the process somewhere. You are going to learn as much on the streets as you will from the books." I often tell people that I wish I could give the books away free and take 10% of what they are going to make from their investments.

Usually you pay under $25 for a book. Even if you only get one idea from the book and it saves you or makes you an extra

$100 on a deal, you have more than paid for your investment. If you go to a seminar that costs you $500 tuition, how many ideas do you need? You are probably going to make that $500 every time you buy. Even if you never buy an investment property, you will make it on your own home.

A man came up to my aide after a seminar and was perusing the literature there. He said, "They sure are charging a lot of money for these books." Another man came up and bought the entire set of books while the first man was standing there. The first man asked, "Is there anything worthwhile in there?"

The second man replied, "Listen, I've been to these things for the last twenty years. I've never spent $300 on a pack of books before, but I can make $3,000 from one good idea."

I'm often asked by seminar attendees about purchasing other speakers' products. I use the same rationalization. What happens if you take this amortization schedule and attach it to your offer and you save $80 a month for the next 28 years while the loan is in existence? $80 a month for 28 years compared to a one-time expense of $145 for this set of tapes is a good investment.

The bottom line is that nothing works until you do. I'm not suggesting that you become a seminar junkie and never go out and make an offer. But these materials are loaded with ideas, and only one idea could make or save you money. It is in your best interest to stay educated and use what you have learned.

I recently heard a beautiful story about a young man who went up to Mozart and said, "Mozart, I would like to have your advice. I'd like to be a composer. Can you tell me how to get started?"

Mozart said, "Well, I think you ought to go back and study, take all the courses you can, and wait a while before you start composing."

The young man said, "Wait a minute, you started composing when you were three years old; why do I have to wait?"

"Because I didn't have to ask anyone how to get started."

One other point: some of those same books and tapes can be given to spouses, attorneys or CPA's to educate them and bring them up to a higher level of competence. Some people have a tendency to resist change, but they need to change because the tax laws change, the state laws change. In fact, nothing ever stays the same.

If people stopped learning as soon as they reached any level of competence, without continuing their education and pushing forward, we would still be living in caves.

Solve People-Problems

Fifth, solve people-problems: with interest rates and terms the way they are today, it is almost impossible to do business with the banks. At the very least, it is a frustrating experience. When interest rates were around 12%, we thought if they dropped there would be a possibility that we could deal with the banking institutions. Now it is "due-on-sale" clauses that keep banks out. However, probably the two most important ideas that work for today are to realize that banks are unreasonable and that money is hard, and it is likely to stay that way.

But Americans still need to buy and sell homes. We sometimes forget that we don't have to walk in and pay cash for everything. There are enough people out there who need to sell their home and who are willing to take monthly payments for their equity. You can save yourself a lot of time before you ever drive out to look at a home by calling the seller on the phone. If you have fifteen prospective houses to buy, call fifteen owners and say, "I notice that you are going to sell your home. Are you willing to take monthly payments for your equity?" If they say no, then just go on to the next one.

By getting acquainted with sellers and their particular needs, you will be able to purchase their property and solve their problems better than any bank could hope to.

Avoid Costly Entanglements

Sixth, avoid costly entanglements: it's okay to make mistakes, but it isn't okay to go into something head-on without examining the possibilities. Avoid unsuspecting partnership ideas, like equity sharing. Think everything through to the end. Think about the entanglements that you will get into with other people. It's simple to say, "Okay, I'll buy the property from you with the following terms." The sellers have a lien on the property, and if you don't fulfill your part of the bargain, they get the property back. It's a simple cut-and-dried thing. There's no partnership involved in that.

Many speakers suggest that you go into partnership with unsophisticated people. One man teaches a seminar and says that the only way you are going to make money is to get all your tenants to go into partnership with you so they will pay a higher rent than average. What happens if the person who owns half of the property right now gets a lien against him and they take your half, too? Remember, in a partnership, they always go for the deeper pockets.

There are many ideas that you should be cautious of. You should only use ideas that feel comfortable to you. You'll see seminar after seminar come through every major city in this country. If you can't picture yourself doing what the seminar is advocating, don't do it. Listen to every lecture, and see if it makes sense to *you*.

Look For A Return On Your Money

Seventh, look for a return on your money: in the 1990s and 21st century it is necessary to look at potential investments in terms of getting your initial investment back. Realistically speaking, you can expect to have some amount of cash outlay in anything you buy, even if it is only closing costs.

So, when you approach a property, you should look at it and ask yourself: "What can I rent this thing for?" Then you ask people in that neighborhood what the houses are renting for there. You could also ask the real estate agents in the area. You should also ask yourself about the sale of that property when it comes time for you to resell it. If you were going for cash flow, as in the Money Machine concept, how much would it sell for? If you were trying to get a cash-out, how much could you sell it for? And, if you were willing to take a note back and carry the financing, how much could you sell it for? We're talking about making money. That's our main goal. That is why it is necessary to explore all the ins and outs of every deal.

Get Involved With Foreclosures

Eighth, get involved with foreclosures: foreclosure properties have always existed, but there are some special circumstances with foreclosures that were created by the economic climate of the 1980s.

High interest rates, due-on-sale clauses, balloon payments, and high monthly payments have created a glut of foreclosures and REO (Real Estate Owned) properties on the market today. The banks are stuck with these properties. Homes are being foreclosed on because homeowners are willing to unload their properties. Some of these will be vacant while the foreclosure process is taking place. If we can get involved in these properties before the bank takes possession, we could find a $70,000 house for $40,000 or $50,000. Instead of being the villain by taking this family's home from them, we can be a hero and save their credit rating. We can purchase these houses usually by making up the back payments before they go to the auction block.

I have written a detailed explanation of this method of purchasing foreclosure properties in my book, *How To Pick Up Foreclosures*, which you can get at any bookstore or by ordering from me directly.

Make A Few Small Mistakes

Ninth, make a few small mistakes: a buyer walked in to a seller and stated: "I was just reading this book and it suggested that I could make you a down payment by giving part of your down payment to you right now and the rest of it in a year, and I could pay you $180 a month for your equity. Would that be okay?"

The seller replied: "No, I need about $250 a month." Now you have the beginning of a deal. You're starting to talk. You have to get out there and make it happen.

You can figure out the process, but you can't figure it out by sitting at home. You figure it out by going out and making a few mistakes. You have to make mistakes. You may as well go and get them out of the way next week so you can get on with making money. Don't be afraid of making mistakes.

Ask Yourself, "What If?"

Tenth, ask yourself, "what if?": life is filled with "what ifs." What if I can't sell this property? What if I become disabled, or what if I lose my job? The handful of successful people do not allow uncertainties to determine how they will live. The only thing that is certain is that nothing is certain, and the only way to beat Murphy is to stay one step ahead of him, every step of the way.

From buying property to taking out life insurance to creating a will to buying medical insurance, we need to understand that we live in a complex society and many things can go wrong. We should be like the farmhand in this old story:

A farmer needed someone to help out around his farm. Asking around, he heard about a farmhand who was available. The farmer asked the man what his qualifications were. "I can sleep when the wind blows," was the answer. That didn't seem like much of an answer, but it was intriguing. The farmer needed the help, and the man had been highly recommended.

The farmer hired the man, and after a couple of months, he decided that his fears were groundless, the man was the best farmhand he had ever seen.

One night the farmer was awakened from a sound sleep by the sound of a raging storm. The wind shrieked and the branches whipped against the bedroom window. Jumping out of bed, he yanked on his overalls and ran to the bunkhouse. The farmhand was sleeping soundly, and the farmer couldn't rouse him. "So this is what he meant when he said he could sleep when the wind blows," cursed the farmer. Rushing out into the night, the farmer ran first to the field. The horses would be frightened, and they would run away when the gate was blown open by the strong winds. But when he got to the field, the gate was wired tightly shut and the horses—although frightened—were safe.

Pushing against the wind, the farmer struggled to the barn, anticipating the worst. But the barn was bolted shut, and all of the animals were inside. There was a tarp drawn across the haystack and tied down. Wherever he looked, the farmer could see that everything had already been secured. And then he really knew what the man meant when he said, "I can sleep when the wind blows."

The farmhand succeeded because he made sure that everything was taken care of before hard times hit. Investors—successful investors—are ready for the unexpected.

Take Risks

Eleventh, take risks: while driving down the street recently, I had to stop at a crosswalk. A half dozen burly road workers were installing a huge new manhole and gutter system. I thought it was so interesting that I pulled over to the side and got out. I walked over to one of the men and talked to him for a while. He thought what they were doing was exciting, but he admitted that the job wasn't much fun because they were working outdoors, and the weather was getting cold.

I realized as I drove away that if he and his coworkers stayed where they were, they would always be able to afford only those things that they could afford right now. It's only by taking risks that any of us are able to break out of our existing situations. So many people have come to seminars lately looking to real estate as a way out of their problems. I encourage that kind of thinking. I want to uncover in them a desire to be more and to do more.

Summary

As I teach and as I write, I don't think that I'm telling people anything new. Perhaps a person who is now forty-five years old is hearing something from me, about something that he had wanted to do, back when he was twenty-two years old and lost that dream because he got bogged down in the mundane affairs of trying to pay the bills.

The problem is that so many of us see the possibilities, but so few of us act. We are excited to get going, but we don't do it. We are literally unable to take the necessary steps to create our own wealth.

After I had been investing for a year and a half, my monthly income was up over $4,400 a month. That is net money that would be coming in for many, many years. A friend was visiting me for three days, and after seeing all the hubbub and activity I was creating, he said, "Wade, you ought to quit all this and get a job," (by the way, this person had never made $4,400 in one month in his life). As Don Berman says, "95% of the advice is given by 95% of the people who aren't making any money." My friend did not understand what I was trying to accomplish by building up my cash flow, my tax write-offs, and my growth for the future. Those areas of real estate investing are phenomenal, and they need action.

You have to realize that you are not competing with a lot of other people; you are just competing with yourself. You're running your own race. You're climbing your own ladder of success. Yes, we all want to make sure that after we climb our ladder of success our ladder will be leaning against the right wall, but we have to get going now, we have to do something now. Don't put off doing something until tomorrow if you can do it today.

If you're a brand new investor, you will have to go through a learning curve. You are going to make mistakes. It's time to get these mistakes out of your way. If you don't buy that property this week, if you don't make an offer on the duplex this week, when are you going to do it? Next week? Some time in the future? You need to do it now and quit putting it off. Quit analyzing to the point of no action. Quit creating so many questions and problems because confusion means "no." Once your mind is confused, it will do nothing. Procrastination is the scourge of any investment. There are always going to be good deals out there. We don't need to take advantage of all the good deals today, but we do need to take advantage of what we can handle today.

Real estate investing is the greatest and most demanding form of investment. As I said before, most fortunes are made with real estate investments, but they are not made by people who are sitting home watching television. They are made by people who are out on the street finding the good deals. They are made by people who work hard for two, three, five, or 10 years, and then, all of a sudden, overnight, they, too, become an "instant success."

CHAPTER 16

HOW TO GET STARTED

In this chapter we're going to take three different people with three different scenarios and go out and start investing in real estate. The first person will be somebody who is working or is possibly out of work, but nevertheless has no money. The second person is somebody who is making good money right now and has between $5,000 and $20,000 to start investing. The third person is somebody who is in a rather high tax bracket, has more than enough to meet his needs right now, and wants to buy real estate for tax purposes.

I would strongly advise readers to look at each section. As I mentioned in a previous chapter, we all go through these three stages. The first stage is the accumulation stage, when we are building our assets and our net income. The second stage is the maintenance stage, when we seek to maintain that which we have built. The third stage is for our retirement. It doesn't matter whether you are twenty years old or eighty years old, everyone is in one of these three stages. In the chapter on leverage, I made a case for buying real estate with very little money. I would like to reiterate one portion of that here. My feeling is that real estate is a great investment because we can buy it with the law of leverage, and the better we get at this law of leverage, the more real estate we can buy.

If people are very wealthy, they are usually in a high tax bracket and should be buying leverage property to create leveraged tax write-offs and to maximize the use of their money that way. It doesn't matter how much money people have, they should be putting as little down in investment real estate as possible. I will not try here to tell how much they should put down if they are buying their own home. This purchase is not an investment, even though it might turn out to be an investment property in later years. Most people do not buy their homes for that reason and are willing to pay more on the purchase price and put up more of a down payment if it is for their personal use. We will restrict our remarks here to investment real estate.

People With No Money

In another section of this book I give many ways of buying real estate with no money. Probably half of the books written about real estate investments deal with this subject, but one of the common problems that I see is that people put the emphasis on the down payments rather than on the monthly payments. I think in today's economy the emphasis should be on the monthly payments that we are agreeing to pay, rather than just on the down payment.

For our first scenario, let me introduce you to David. David is twenty years old. He is very ambitious and doesn't want to follow the trade of his father. He wants to start investing. He stumbled across a seminar and learned that he could get started investing in real estate even while he was in college. The most he could scrape together was $400, which is probably not even enough to pay the closing costs in many of the areas around the country. The tactic that David used was to find a house that needed fixing up and one on which he could do the work himself. The property that he found was a $50,000 to $55,000 property that he found for $45,000. His offer to the seller of the property was $42,000, and they countered back at $43,000. They wanted to have $4,000 to pay some bills, and he offered to pay them $2,000. They accepted because they needed to unload the property, and it needed more fixing up than they had the time or the money to do. But David did not have the $2,000.

What I would like to do here is give several different alternatives for coming up with the $2,000. One way would be to find loan money from a credit union or bank or other kind of lending institution. A second way would be to borrow the money from a family member or a friend, and a third way would be to find somebody who might want to get involved in the property as a partner. This person could be a dentist or doctor, or an attorney to someone David might know. What he did do was to ask the people if he could give them $2,500 in three months. This was going to seriously affect what they wanted to do because they needed the money right away, but they agreed to do this if he would promise them that he would try to get them the money before the three months were up. He agreed to do so. His money and a little of their money had to go into the closing costs, and the deal was signed. They moved out of the property, which solved one of their problems, and he was able to go in and start working on the property because he had accounts set up at hardware, paint, and other kinds of stores where he could buy materials to fix up his property.

Immediately he was able to get $1,000 worth of materials and start fixing up the house. On this house he wanted to do a Money Machine sale, and he put it up for sale almost immediately (while he was fixing it up), for $53,000, with $4,000 down and he would carry back the paper. However, as so often happens, someone came in and offered $7,000 and agreed to take over his $41,000 loan. He was able to then take $2,500 out of the $7,000 and pay the original sellers their money. He also recovered the $1,000 he already had in fix-up costs. He was able to do this before the house was even fixed up. The people were, in fact, buying it for $48,000 when he was trying to sell it for $53,000. They got a tremendous deal and were able to finish fixing it up the way they wanted to. He was able to walk away with over $4,000 in his pocket for three weeks' work.

Once this is done, it can be repeated. There are several other angles to keep going. But even though he now has a little money to invest further, if he pretends he doesn't have the money and goes back and makes a similar transaction on another property and does this once or twice a month or every other month, you can see the money that he would make. On the next house he may want to hold the house as rental property, and on the third house he may want to quickly sell it once again. Once people have $3,000 to $4,000, they're off and running because there are many things that can be done with that little amount of money.

People with No Time

Our second scenario describes a person who is too busy to invest in real estate. He is working at a full-time job, making good money, has a little spendable income but just doesn't have the inclination to go out and look under houses and coordinate putting up sheet rock and get the painting done. This is the situation that most investors find themselves in, and it's one I've been in almost since the first year of investing. Even when I was actively investing in real estate, I realized that there were other angles of real estate investment I needed to be involved in. One of the easiest things that I found to do was to hire somebody to work for me. My basic format was that I would pay people between $800 to $1,200 a month and give them $100 every time they bought a property and $100 every time they sold the property. These people could easily make $20,000 to $30,000 a year and gain a great deal of experience.

The one pitfall was that I was training my best competitors. It got to the point that I would sign an agreement with them so that they wouldn't go into competition with me within a couple of hundred miles from where we were investing. I was using their services as an employee, but one of the reasons they wanted to come to work for me was they could get the knowledge and experience and then go off and do it on their own, which I heartily endorsed. But in any city there are only so many good deals, and I didn't want to take two or three people on and show them all of my tactics for investing in a certain neighborhood and then two weeks later find them out buying the houses out from under me.

What these people can do for you will be exactly what you would do if you weren't so busy. You obviously should look at the deals before anything is closed and signed. You'll have to squeeze out a couple of hours to check over the closing documents to make sure that everything is right. When they find a house or any kind of investment property, you will want them to give you pertinent information that would be vital to your decision making. I remember a time when I had someone working for me. He called me on the phone and said, "Oh, wow, Wade, I found this great house in the Parkland area."

I said, "Good, tell me about the financing."

He said "Man, you should see it. It's got fourteen fruit trees," and I said, "Good, tell me about the financing."

"Wow, it has great new wallpaper in the kitchen and new kitchen cabinets," he said.

I said, "That's nice, tell me about the financing."

He said, "You ought to see the upstairs, big bedrooms, cedar closets in all the bedrooms," and I said, "Tell me about the financing." You shouldn't care about any of these other things until you find out if you can buy the property or not.

Here are some pertinent questions that should be asked, and, by the way, these questions are on the Property Analysis sheet found at the end of this book. This is what I want to know:

- What are the balances on the loan? Are the loans assumable?

- How much equity do they have?

- What are they asking for the house and how long has the house been up for sale?

- How much down payment do they want? When do they want the down payment? Can they take part of it now and part of it later?

- What do they want for the rest of the equity? Do they need cash or are they willing to take monthly payments, or are they willing to take a note for the balance of their equity at some future date?

- Is there an agent involved?

- What about their commissions?

- What are they willing to do?

- How much fixing up is it going to take? Once the fixing up is done, what will it rent for?

- Is it rented now? Have the rents been raised lately?

- What are the different possibilities for purchasing the house?

- Can we purchase it for $55,000 with $5,000 down? How about $58,000 with $3,000 down, or $62,000 with nothing down?

I want my employees to give me this kind of information, and if I am the one looking at the house or talking with the people on the phone about the house, I should get the answers to these questions. I have to know the different possibilities so I can make a wise decision from a basis of different alternatives.

Having people working for you can be a great asset because not only can they help with collection of rents, but they can also run all the errands for you and help you to accomplish the little things that you just don't have time to do. One of my friends has an employee at $5 an hour checking at the courthouse every day to see if there are any notices of defaults posted. He sends out six to ten letters a day to people who are starting into the foreclosure process. He wants to get the house in the very early stages. It would be too tedious, and an unwise use of his time, to do the work himself, but if he can hire somebody at an hourly rate to do it, then he is once again maximizing his own time.

Another alternative for the busy person is to do it part time. Most investors start this way. By no means is this the easiest way, but sometimes it is the only alternative. It is tough to squeeze out a couple of nights a week and a couple of weekends a month to look for properties and to do the necessary fixing up. It isn't very much fun once several rental properties are purchased. It seems people can spend all of their time trying to collect the rents. If they find themselves in this busy state, they are definitely going to have to leverage their time and leverage other people. For example, if they buy property and hold it for a rental property they might want to find a property manager. They may now also be at an income stage where they should be considering investing in limited partnerships: they put up all the money, and somebody else does all the work. The rate of return may not be as high, but sometimes that doesn't matter when they are busy in their career.

All the principles we have talked about in this book apply to any of the angles. It is better if people who are going to actively invest in real estate have time during the normal business hours to be available to check out properties and to talk with the people involved in the closing process to make sure that everything runs smoothly. I've often contended that it takes about 40% of your energy to find the property, about 20% of your energy to walk through the deal, and 40% of your energy to rustle it through the closing to make sure that everything happens when and how it's supposed to happen.

There are really no secrets to success. The principles of successful investing are the same. If people do it part time, they will just have to do it more slowly than if they were doing it full time and using all of their energy during normal business hours. But success can still be realized if it is put in perspective. People making $60,000 a year might find themselves living comfortably. They need investments for tax write-offs. These people may have to buy four or five investment properties this year, which may be really hard, but they will offset for tax purposes that $60,000 income. Whether the properties are making any money may be irrelevant because cash flow at this point just causes more problems. A few properties can stop that tax drain.

People with Money

Our third scenario involves someone with a lot of money. Let's also assume that the tax bracket is rather high. We will not need a lot of razzle-dazzle in this case. The hustle to make the money is completed. Now it's time to keep growing, and, at the same time, reduce the tax liability.

If we're past the stage where there's a strong need for cash flow, it will be relatively easy. Let's assume a taxable income of $100,000. Normal deductions will account for $10,000 (including dependents, donations, and other write-offs). What needs to be sheltered, then, is $90,000.

It is very common to hear things like a 2-to-1 write-off or a 2.7-to-1 tax shelter. Simply put, 2-to-1 means that for every dollar you put up, you're getting two dollars in deductions. If you're in a 50% tax bracket, you can deduct the two dollars from your income and save exactly one dollar.

Let's see how this works in our example. We invest $10,000 in a legitimate money-making enterprise. The investment also has write-offs this year of $20,000. We deduct this amount from our $90,000 and actually save the taxes that we would have paid on the extra $20,000 of income.

Let's say we find a unit building for $240,000. The land is valued at $40,000, and we depreciate the remaining $200,000. Using ACRS, and by depreciating the appliances and furnishings, we get a $20,000 write-off. If we had put up $20,000, it would be a 1:1 write-off. If we had purchased it for $10,000 down, then it would be a 2:1 write-off. It gets interesting if we put less down, but it's very difficult to find anything less than 5% down. A $5,000 down payment would be a 4:1 write-off, and absolutely nothing down would be infinity. Remember, you can't divide by zero.

I mention all of this because we all need to measure our money. The yield is important. Figured into the yield would be the cash flow (or lack of it) and could be the growth.

From a tax point of view, investments are measured this way. It bothers me that people selling investments rely so heavily on this fact. What about the property? Is it going to make money? I strongly suggest that you look for the best investments. An investment shouldn't be good only because you happen to be in a 50% bracket.

But I'm also a realist. If you make a lot of money and you can get a legitimate 4-to-1 write-off and save a lot on your taxes, the tax angle alone could make it well worth your time to invest. Make sure you study it and that reputable firms recommend it.

Active Versus Passive

You can probably tell that I'm talking about a passive form of investment in most of the preceding paragraphs—*passive* meaning that you put up the money and nothing else. Someone else does all the work.

An active form of investing would require the work and the money by you. There are so many good investments today in the form of partnerships. Once again, I recommend real estate. The write-offs are higher in non-real-estate limited partnerships, but there are too many red flags.

As discussed in the chapter on taxes, if you create enough losses (actual or paper) to offset this year's income, you can apply any excess losses to the last three years' income. You can then take it 15 years into the future and offset income as you earn it. Also you don't have to go back if you didn't make very much the past three years and plan on making a lot more in the future. One last point on this: many people pay quarterly estimated taxes. Don't forget your estimated quarterly losses. If you start making more money, just buy a few more properties and alleviate your tax liability.

Will you get audited with all these losses? Probably not. Most IRS agents work on a quota system. They have to justify their existence by collecting so much money. Naturally they will go after the easiest prey. Real estate paper losses are so common and so justified by law that once they see a property address, they'll put it down and go on to someone investing in oil.

A sad situation has developed lately. Many Americans find themselves getting very prosperous. Almost every book or newsletter for them is self-serving. I get seemingly good advice from a company one day, and then I'm chosen by the same company to be among a special few to buy a British-minted special edition silver coin. Most books on estate planning and tax shelters have no excitement and are either so basic or so complicated that they are worthless.

My chapter in this book on income splitting is a fair start, but because this book is written for the general public, I can't get too specific. I act like a traffic cop and just point the way. If you like what I write and would like more information on estate planning, tax shelters, wealthy investment tactics, and the like, please write or call. I have an entire seminar and an entire audio cassette tape set on these strategies, which will save you thousands of dollars.

Most of us don't have the knowledge or the time to study everything. If an investment is presented to you, make sure you have people around you to help you out. Some are very exciting while others are very technical; there are also many CPAs and attorneys who specialize in these.

Summary
Whether you're poor, on the way up, or have arrived, protect your growth and your success with real estate. Nothing grows as fast as real estate, and nothing protects your growth as well as real estate.

And to truly protect yourself from lawsuits and taxes of all kinds, call 1-800-872-7411 (or write to Wade Cook Seminars, Inc., 14675 Interurban Avenue South, Seattle, Washington, 98168-4664) and ask about the Financial Fortress audio cassette series, or the three-day Wealth Academy Seminar. These resources teach you specific ways to legally pay less or no taxes.

CHAPTER 17

INCOME SPLITTING

Necessity is the mother of invention. So much of what I accomplished in my early years of investing was done by hit or miss; the try, back up, and try-again method. I sometimes wondered if I would ever get ahead. Luckily, though, the information I needed to continue the process of achieving my goals was available.

As I started having some success in one area, it seemed that problems would crop up in other areas. Many a good book was written to get people started investing and to give the "how to's" of putting certain deals together. Once in a while, these books would show the results of such knowledge and effort. Often, when I needed information, I could go to a book or to a professional and get the specific help I needed.

But it became apparent that even after achieving a modest amount of success, I would soon need a comprehensive system of investing in real estate, a system that had solutions to these problems:

- Generating and maintaining positive cash flows

- Sheltering income through long-term installment sales and depreciation expense

- Providing security for the future

- Keeping current income (cash) working for the three previous problems without being swallowed in the IRS abyss

- Finding a way of working hard for a while, then with relative ease, slowing down and using only a small amount of time and energy

- Directing assets to beat inflation

Sound like a tall order? It was just that. But I realized right away that maintaining assets is almost as hard as building them up. So I had no alternative but to find a plan that worked.

Obviously, there were no college courses for the real estate investor to take (See more information about my Real Estate Workshop in the resource section at the back of this book). Yes, there are books and seminars available, and I encourage reading and taking as many of these as possible. However, what is really needed is more comprehensive than any one or two of these. Don't get me wrong. I'm not putting down attempts to buy with no money down, or the idea of papering your way to millions, or equity participation, or any of the other strategies that rise and fall in popularity. All of these are good as stepping stones. They should be viewed as tools, and it is well known how important it is to have the most modern, up-to-date tool chest possible. Once successful, I wasn't in need of specific techniques, but a whole system.

I've spent these past few paragraphs trying to get us all on the same footing. What will be explained now is an A to Z system for investing in real estate that encompasses these good, honest methods and puts them to work for your financial security.

The Start of the System
I was becoming quite successful with my properties and started worrying about my long- and short-term tax liabilities. It was to answer this tax question that I started the search for a "total concept."

One lesson I have had to learn too many times was to concentrate my energies on one thing. Many of the popular non-real-estate tax shelter ideas weren't good for me. My expertise was growing with small properties, and I wanted to capitalize on my knowledge and experience. There was no time to start over in a different field.

I spent one afternoon listening to an insurance agent/investment counselor expound the virtues of tax shelter investment opportunities. I tried to find the good. I tried hard. But when I compared his annual investment returns with my weekly and monthly returns, they couldn't compare. I would do better to keep my money working and just pay the taxes.

He then listened to me for a while. He could see what I had accomplished and the growth I was having, and he candidly told me I needed a corporate pension and profit-sharing plan (hereinafter called the Plan). Hungry for new information, I pressed him for more. What he told me was almost too good to be true.

Before we get into the specifics of the Plan, let me first mention that you need to incorporate to put more money each year into the Plan. A Nevada corporation is the best. Contact Wade Cook Seminars at 1-800-872-7411 for information on setting up a Nevada Corporation.

As many of you know from reading my books and articles, I had devised a system for finding really good deals, then selling them on a wraparound basis in an attempt to recover my down payment and fix-up cost so I could do it again; build up a strong net income from turning many properties this way; and spread out my tax liabilities over the twenty-five to thirty years of the wraparound mortgage by claiming my gain on the installment sales method.

This plan worked well and became the income generation part of the whole system. Also, the creation of this plan let me move on to a surer way of protecting my assets and helped me learn how to invest in several types of properties and transactions.

I left the agent's office as excited about what he had told me as anything I've ever been excited about. I immediately made an appointment with my attorney to check it all out.

Let me give you the gist of what the Plan can do so you can see how it fits into the picture. Once incorporated, you use your corporation to buy and sell properties. It needs to start fresh and go out and make a profit. This can be done by any of the techniques you've learned. It can buy with zero down; it can lease option properties; it can form equity participation agreements; it can assume old FHA and VA loans. In short, it can do what you can do. It is a legal entity with a life of its own.

It's easy to get it started. Once done, you just buy properties in the corporation's name. If you are new at this, it would be advisable to seek competent, professional help. Do it right so you can avoid headaches later on.

Now that the corporation is operating on its own and making a profit, it can take 25% (or more with certain Plans) of the money available for wages and put it into the Plan. What is this "money available for salary?" It's not the net profit that is calculated after taking out the salary. *It is only the money paid out in salary* For example, let's say your corporation made $80,000 gross by turning six properties this year. Let's say the costs of doing business total $20,000. You now subtract the $20,000 from the $80,000 and that leaves $60,000 available for salaries. Perhaps your salary to yourself and a few employees totals $45,000. The 25% would then be on the $45,000 paid out, which comes to $11,250. That's $11,250 that can be put into the Plan.

This donation to the Plan becomes an immediate tax write-off to the corporation. So now the corporation pays less taxes. As a matter of fact, continuing with the same example, our $80,000 gross income is lessened by the $20,000 expenses, the $45,000 in salaries and the $15,000 in donations to the Plan. That leaves zero income to the corporation, which means *no tax liability.*

What is the Pension and Profit-Sharing Plan? It's a separate legal entity set up and recognized by the IRS for the benefit of the retirement of the employees of your corporation.

It is a trust that is a living, thriving entity. It can do so many things, and the real beauty is that you can be the trustee and control where the money is to be invested.

Where does the money go? It goes into the Plan's checking or savings account. It is then available for investing. You, as the trustee, decide what types of properties it will buy (or sell). It can buy rentals, fixer uppers, discounted mortgages, lots for developing, or even investing stocks, bonds, gold, or any other business. In short, it can do what you can do, but with one major exception. All of the money in the Plan can be turned over time and time again. The Plan can buy and sell and make thousands and thousands of dollars—it can even grow into millions—tax free. The Plan will never pay taxes.

What happens to this money? It just stays in the Plan investing or earning interest until you decide to retire. Let's say you turn 44 or whatever age and declare your retirement. You begin to take out $3,000 a month to live on. You will now have to claim that income as it is taken out and claim it in your then current tax bracket (you'll then need to buy a few rental properties or tax shelters to create enough depreciation expense to even offset this amount).

I've just given the highlights here. Sound good? It's the greatest tax shelter I've ever seen, and the Plan I've just described (Purchase Money Plan) is the least of the three available (Defined Benefit and Defined Contribution—ask a pension and profit-sharing plan administrator for details).

Let's see what others are doing. Managers of large pension funds across the United States are turning their attention back to real estate in a big way, according to a recent article in the *Wall Street Journal.* According to the article, the number of pension fund advisory firms specializing in real estate has grown from six, in the 70s to 150 in the 80s and more today.

Real estate was either an impractical or forbidden investment for most pension funds back around 1970, that is, until Prudential Insurance Company of America bought a variety of properties. That was the beginning.

The idea really started to gain momentum in 1977-78. The stock market was down, inflation was very much on the rise, and real estate was a "hot" item.

Today pension funds are believed to have invested $100 billion in real estate. One consulting firm estimates that this will continue to grow.

After a slackening off in 1981 and 1982, real estate began to pick up again. Prudential Insurance Company reports that contributions to its largest real estate account rose 1600% in one year.

This is just another testimony to what real estate can do for you, the individual investor, today. Now is the time to invest. The big guys aren't hesitating.

Three Entities

Over the years I've developed the three entity approach to investing in real estate. The three entities are the corporation, the individual, and the pension and profit-sharing plan. Don't let this sound complicated. I firmly believe in keeping things simple. This whole system has simplicity at its core and has a goal of progressing rapidly in the present while setting up a foundation for long-term wealth accumulation and retention.

The corporation's main objective is twofold. It is the entity that makes profits to pay me a salary and to put the money into the Plan as a tax write-off. Its income comes from capital gains and interest income generated on the loans (mortgages, deeds of trust, and so on) that you create or buy and then carry. By effectively paying out all of its income, the corporation has no tax liability.

The individual has a main objective of eating and sleeping comfortably. You and I both need just to live—to pay our bills. With the excess salary received from the corporation, we invest in income-producing properties that create the depreciation expense and NOL (Net Operating Loss) to offset this same income (and possibly income in other tax years) thereby not paying any taxes.

The Plan's goal is to grow at a rate faster than the other two can grow and provide income and security for our future. The three work together. Once the three entities are in place (and it could take two to three months to set them up), you are ready to grow faster than you've ever thought possible. If handled right, none of the entities will have to pay taxes—leaving all of your cash available for more investing. Isn't that exciting? You'll once again feel as if you're back in control.

Let's see how they work together on a specific deal. When the earnest money agreement (offer to purchase) is signed, you, as the purchaser, should be "John D. and Mary J. Doe, husband and wife, or their assigns . . ." Your offers should have this so you can assign the transactions to either the corporation or to the Plan on or before closing the transaction. You'll not always know which one of your entities should be buying the property, and this will give you time to decide.

Which one *will* buy it? That depends on several things. I firmly believe in not leaving money tied up in a property. I don't want my cash to become equity. If the deal requires a down payment and fix-up costs, then I want either the corporation or the Plan to buy it. I turn and sell this type of property, and I want the profits (probably short-term capital gain) to be in one of these two entities.

Which one of the two should receive the profits? That depends on which one has money at the time, or which one I'm actively working with at the moment. Obviously, I would like to be spending all of my time developing the tax-free asset growth of the Plan, but I need to live, so the corporation needs to continue to create an income. Yes, the need to be actively working the corporate assets will go down as it creates more and more steady income, but at the beginning you'll have to look closely at which entity will do the buying.

If the purchase requires little or no money down and very few repairs and has a positive or break-even cash flow, then the property is a prime candidate to be held for the long term. I buy this property as an individual. This lets me 1) take advantage of the depreciation expense and 2) sell it and take advantage of long-term capital gains.

Buying long-term rental properties and selling only once in a while keeps my investment status as an investor and not a dealer. The properties that will be turned right away can go under the corporation or the Plan.

As I mentioned before, this is a whole system of growth. The beauty is the *no tax,* rapid growth aspects. And the whole system can be done with any business that you're in. Real estate works so well and is a natural for the three entities because of the income generation attribute, the growth potential, and the tax shelter aspect already there to enhance each of the entities.

And because it is a complete system, any of the entities can use any of the techniques of buying fix-up, holding, and selling of real estate. Indeed, the three entity approach gives new life to many of these techniques. They are the tools you need to start and maintain your own investment system.

CHAPTER 18

MONEY, MONEY, MONEY

A short while ago I was interviewed on a national TV show on investments, called "Money, Money, Money" with host Hal Morris. Because it recapitulates so much of what I'm writing about in the book, I'll include a modified transcription of the show here.

HAL: Wade is one of the hottest lecturers and authors in the United States today. He's come up with some ideas on how you can avoid using banks and how it makes sense to turn around and sell rather than hold real estate. Wade goes against much of the traditional wisdom, and today he's going to be sharing his ideas with us.

First of all, you were a taxi driver. You have gone through some of the processes that the average person has gone through and come up with some solutions. Tell us your story.

WADE: Well, I was driving a taxi, and I had read a few books on real estate. I wanted to get started, but I didn't have very much money. I had only a little money for a down payment and to fix up one house. But I started investing, and I ended up buying nine houses the first year with taxi money. But then I realized that just owning property doesn't make very much sense if it doesn't mean anything in monthly income. I came up with the idea of selling one of my houses, but the house I wanted to sell wouldn't qualify for bank financing. So a friend said, "Well, why don't you sell it on contract?" (Now we don't use contracts. We use wraparound mortgages or all inclusive trust deeds.)

I said, "What's a contract?" He said, "You take a small down payment from the guy and then he makes you monthly payments." I said, "Really? Can I do that?" He said, "Sure!" So I went down to a title company and told them what I'd learned about contracts and asked if I could do that sort of thing. They said, "Yes, we do it all the time." They did it. It cost me $180. They drew up all the papers, typed up everything, did the recording, and even collected the payments for me, and sent me a check for $80. Well, later on I had another property that wouldn't qualify for bank financing. I sold it the same way. I was making $60. I stopped and thought, "This is kind of neat. I'm not a landlord, I'm not collecting rents from people, they are making me the payments. I got my down payments back." See, when I sold them I not only received my down payment—I received excess down payments back. I sat there and said, "This is really neat! Forget the rentals and forget the banks, this is too much fun." So what I did was start buying and selling properties and creating notes on all these different properties. I worked about thirty-four houses my first year.

HAL: That's exciting. So that's just like a little money machine? Every time you did one, there was money coming in?

WADE: Right. The average monthly payment coming to me was $95 a month. I had one that was $8, and my best one was $290. But my average was $95 a month.

HAL: And now you've got that income coming for 15, 20, 25 years?

WADE: It can come in for about 23 to 25 years, but they all cash out after four, five, or six years, because the person that you sold the house to will usually finance through a bank somewhere down the line and cash you out. The neat thing was that I was recycling the original down payment I received. I didn't have any money. I couldn't afford to buy anything when I first started.

HAL: So what you were doing was taking a two or three thousand dollar down payment, getting that money back and creating an incoming stream for yourself?

WADE: Well, I started by borrowing $500 from my father for my first house. I was making a little bit of extra money driving a cab, and when I started investing, I did everything that everyone else was doing in real estate, only I did it backward. They were all saying buy and hold on forever. I'm saying buy and get rid of that thing by Friday.

First of all, we need to find good values. We want to find a property that is way under market value—maybe one that needs fixing up, one that the buyer wouldn't have the money to spend on that sort of thing. Do a little fixing up and build some equity into it, but guard your cash. There is just no way the average person can keep going in real estate by burying monthly payments into the houses he buys.

HAL: Wade, let's get into the elimination of banks. Many people out there do not have financial statements or credit ratings. What can they do to eliminate banks?

WADE: Let's get even more specific. How do you get a loan through a bank being a cab driver? See, I couldn't do anything right at first. Banks want to control every-thing. The interest rates are too high, the monthly payments are too high, and they'll tell you who you can and can't sell to. It's incredible how much control they have.

I made the decision about four and a half years ago to never use a bank again. I don't think we need them in the real estate industry. They cause more problems than they solve (there are many people out there who see problems we can solve). We sure can't solve the banks' problems. So four and a half years ago, I said, "That's it. No more banks." I'm being facetious. I go in and I get cashier's checks and make deposits. I just have a real hard time with bankers, and so what I did was set up a system.

I looked around and said, "How can I do this without using bankers?" The answer was that when I want to buy houses, the first thing I want to do is assume the existing loans so that when I want to sell, I can keep making payments on the existing loans. If there are due-on-sale clauses or similar kinds of clauses, I don't have anything to do with them. I am too busy making money to deal with banks. There are four kinds of loans I go tracking down: older FHA, pre-1987 VA, pre-1978 bank loans, and any kind of owner financing.

Let's go back to the first one, the FHA loan. There are no assumption points or anything. There is a name-change fee, and anyone can do it. You could be bankrupt yesterday and assume a FHA loan today. They are easy. They're assumable. I can assume it today, and you can assume it from me tomorrow. You don't even have to be a human being. You don't even have to have a pulse rate. A corporation can assume a FHA loan. When I take a loan over, they won't bump up the interest rate or the monthly payment. If I ever want to pay it off, there's no prepayment penalty clause. You'll look at these and say "Wow, that is so neat! Why would I ever want to do business with any other kind of loan?"

If I'm a beginning investor, yes, it might take me two or three weeks to track down an old FHA loan, but I would probably spend two or three weeks talking to a banker about a due-on-sale clause.

When I teach my seminars around the country, about half of the people take that seriously. I am saying, "Look, the money is in those old FHA and VA loans."

HAL: And there are millions of them out there?

WADE: Out there all over the place.

HAL: And you have had students who have taken your system and gone out and literally made hundreds of thousands of dollars?

WADE: We don't even count anymore. My system says this: let's buy and sell and keep recycling that down payment. If you want to make $2,000 a month, you will need about twenty properties. If you want to make a million dollars and have about $9,000 or $10,000 a month coming in, it will take about eighty or ninety properties, and that's just the way it works. If you only want to make $200 or $300, it will only take a couple of properties. What we are saying is that the old systems are nice, but they are almost archaic to the point of being dangerous. People get into these properties and they think that just because they own real estate they are making all this money.

I talked to one lady in Denver and she said, "I have a million and a half dollars in real estate." I said, "That's great. How much do you make each month?" She said, "Well, if everyone pays their rent, $148." It just doesn't make sense to own that much real estate for that little money.

People buy real estate for three reasons: cash flow, tax shelters, or growth for the future. If you look at the motivation behind the investors out there, you will find that they are all after one of those three things. And the beginning investor is usually after all three.

The biggest reason is cash flow. At my seminars I look at everyone and say, "What is the alternative to cash flow? It's ugly. If you don't have cash flow, you're just flat out stuck." The whole Money Machine system is a cash-flow system. It's a way of putting your money into building a note—putting your money in, getting it back out, and building notes and mortgages. And it's so neat because it's one plan. I don't believe in any complicated formulas. I have a $3.95 calculator from K-Mart. I don't use any complicated formulas. I am buying low and selling just below high. We're just using the American Dream to turn properties.

HAL: What would you say is the biggest mistake people are making out there? You have the people who are the doers and the people who are not succeeding. What do you think most of them are doing wrong?

WADE: I think the number one mistake is that people are putting too much money into real estate. Not only is real estate good for the three reasons I just mentioned, but real estate is good because of all the leverage it offers. You can take $5,000 and buy a $100,000 property, or you can take nothing and buy the same property. Now the song that I want to sing around the country is not the nothing-down, zero-down song. I like it though because it allows you to get in light so you can get out light, and getting out is where all the money is. If you can get in light, you can turn around and sell it and make it a good deal for the next person. The problem is that people want to stick all their money into properties. They put it into down payments, excess monthly payments, and fixing up.

The higher the emotional level, the lower the intellectual level. The way you get emotionally involved is to put all your money into fixing up a place and then discover you want to move in. If you bury your money, it's gone. It's just that way in real estate. Your money's gone. You stick it in and it's gone.

Now, to answer your question specifically: a lot of people say, "If you buy a property and do this and this and this for thirteen years, you'll be a millionaire." I think, "Thirteen years!" How many of us are going to get discouraged? That's long, hard work. I ask people in my seminars how many want to wait thirteen years. Not one hand goes up. I ask how many want to work thirteen months. This Money Machine system, to be a millionaire, takes about eighteen to twenty-two months. That's what it takes. This is not a get-rich-quick scheme. It is a get-rich-slow scheme. It's going to take you eighteen months. We just literally have hundreds of people right now that are doing this one simple little plan. You buy and sell and turn it. We get letters every day from people who are doing it. They are taking all the other great ideas that people have taught them and are saying, "Let's capitalize on them. Let's realize our profits now. Let's get these things sold, take that little bit of money and get on with it again."

HAL: One of the things you have done to accelerate the process is that you encourage them to get involved in foreclosures. In fact, you teach a whole portion of your seminar on foreclosures.

WADE: That's right, and foreclosures can be the key. Now again, remember I was a cab driver. I never had very much money. When I teach about foreclosures, I emphasize the need to get a property way back at the beginning of the foreclosure process. I've never had the cash to get them at the auction block or at the banks afterward. I had to get them when I could pick them up for $3,000 or $5,000 in back payments. On most of my little houses I was making $5,000 to $8,000. On my foreclosure houses I was making $5,000 to $35,000, while saving people's credit ratings, helping them out—it's very exciting. No matter what any real estate investor is doing, foreclosures will enhance it.

HAL: So that will just accelerate the overall system, right? What realistically do you think an income stream could be if someone would come to your three-day seminar and then apply the steps in your system? What kind of income could they turn?

WADE: Well, all I can do is go from past experience. It takes people about three or four months to get their feet wet. It is like any other business. So I tell people, "Look, why make real estate anything other than what it is? It's a business. If you began as a produce manager at a Safeway store, what would you do? You'd learn how to stack cucumbers, learn what good prices are, and learn what good values are. You'd learn what you need to know to do a good job." Well, real estate is the same thing, so you need to know what to do and get your feet wet.

Now the reason that I wrote my books, and the reason I teach seminars is to give people a taste so they can see what it's all about. They need to know what to look for in the newspapers and what kind of deals to go out and look for and lock down. They need to know how to sell them as well as what documents and clauses that they will need to use. So it's still going to take someone two or three months of trying it and testing it on various properties before they can get up to the three-or four-properties-a-month level.

AUDIENCE QUESTIONS AND ANSWERS:

QUESTION: Wade, I need my thinking changed. All my life I have been thinking that it is right to hold real estate for years and get the long-term capital gains. Evidently, that is clear out of your mind. You buy it and sell it and pay your tax and move on.

ANSWER: I like real estate for a tax shelter. I think there is no greater tax shelter in the world. The simple fact that you own enough pieces of property allows you to not pay any taxes. My contention is this: for every $10,000 of income you make, you need one good rental property—like an $80,000 to $100,000 piece of property—and you'll pay no taxes. Now, that's all fine and dandy—later. When the person has the $30,000, $40,000 to $50,000 a year income that they need to offset, then they can buy all the real estate that they want. Now, we have found with the Money Machine concept of turning properties, it is about seven and one. If you turn seven you need one good rental property. Then you never pay any income taxes. Now, the other point is this, when I sell a property on the Money Machine concept, because it is on the installment sales method, the IRS lets me claim my profits as I receive them (if I wrap a property for twenty-three or twenty-five years, I get to take in payments for twenty-three or twenty-five years). You have to claim the interest now, but you get to spread out your profit over the twenty-five years. You can create a large net worth and hardly pay any income tax on the gain because of the installment sales computation.

QUESTION: But at present it's all regular income?

ANSWER: Here's what we're doing in today's market. We like to buy a property with very little money down and sell it on a lease option. Someone can buy it from us fifteen months from now, and that means we go long-term with it, and we get the long-term capital gains. Now, in my seminars and in my book we cover this because I'm trying to show people that they first need to build cash flow and then go for the tax shelters later. Once you have $2,000, $3,000, $4,000 or $5,000 a month coming in, you can go buy all the tax shelters you need. We need to concentrate at first on this one system of building cash flow.

QUESTION: When you sell on a wraparound or an AITD, are you legally responsible for the loan, and if you are, with all of these contracts out there, isn't it risky?

ANSWER: I've put together many of these, and I've never had to foreclose on anyone. When I buy and assume all the underlying loans, I am responsible for them. Now, one of the reasons I like to sell on a wraparound is simply this: If I buy a house for $42,000 with $2,000 down, and now sell it for $52,000 with $2,000 down, I receive my down payment back. They owe me the whole $50,000, and I continue to owe the $40,000. I have had people not make the payments, but I've never had to foreclose. Maybe I've been lucky. One time I was teaching a seminar and a lady said, "Wade, do you think that the reason you have never had to foreclose on anyone is because you might have been that person's only chance at buying a house?" I bet she's right because most of the people wouldn't qualify for bank financing, but they qualify for my financing. They'll hang onto that house for all they're worth.

Yes, it's a little bit risky, but what is the difference when you start with nothing? I have sold these houses, and only one of them turned bad. What is the alternative? The alternative is to sit at home and do nothing and keep hating your existing job.

QUESTION:

What method do you use when you're selling one of these properties? Do you do your own advertising? Do you use a real estate agent? What is your method?

ANSWER:

When I first started this plan, I didn't do anything right. I used to make 14 mistakes a day. Now I've tried to put it all in my book so people don't have to make the same mistakes I've made.

I put myself in the selling business, not in the buying business. The only reason I buy real estate is so that I have something to sell. Once you learn this plan you will be good at rentals or anything else you want to do. I concentrate on trying to find buyers before I find houses. I put ads in the newspaper, and I pass out flyers. I'm an old life insurance agent; I play the numbers game. Whatever it takes to make a successful business, I will do. I used real estate agents many times when I bought but not when I sold because I was so good at selling myself. The average time that I own a house from the time I buy it to the time I sell it is three weeks. Once I have it ready to go, the average time I have it for sale is about four days. The reason I'm able to do it quickly is because it is a good deal for the next person. I'm buying it very low and still selling it below market. I'm selling houses today at $8^1/_2$ to $9^1/_4$%—very good interest rates with low monthly payments. It's such a good deal for the next person that they tell all their friends about it, and I have people waiting in line to buy my houses.

Put the emphasis on selling, not buying. It's amazing what good deals you can find to buy that you can turn around and sell right away.

HAL: Tell them about the business card concept that you came up with.

WADE: My business card just said, "I buy and sell houses." I used to give out 1,000 cards a week. I walked into a printer one time and said, "I want 5,000 business cards." He said, "Are you sure you don't want 500?" I said, "No, I'm thinking big. I want 5,000." I gave them to everybody everywhere I went. I talk to people and they want to be a success. I say, "Okay, how many people know that you are a real estate investor?" Can you count them all on one hand? One finger? Your husband or wife? You need to have 10,000 or 50,000 people out there knowing that you are a real estate investor. Put ads in the paper, pass out flyers, do anything to let people know that you are willing to come out and buy their house.

HAL: Thank you, Wade. It's been great having you on the show.

CHAPTER 19

MAKE IT REAL FOR YOU

Almost every form of investment is fun if you make money at it. There are few people I know who are not tickled when they see their assets growing and their assets and income outpacing inflation. It's exciting and easy to stay enthusiastic.

Why is having fun important? Because the work that is necessary to buy, hold onto, and sell real estate can sometimes get tedious. Sometimes problems become overwhelming, but even at its best, there is a constant need to stay motivated. If an investor lapses into discouragement, time elapses and can't be retrieved.

We've all been there, and we all know how much better we perform when we're excited about something. Sometimes the sheer excitement carries us over the few rough times. If we're excited, we'll do better, and doing better is what it's all about.

Why Real Estate?

There are several reasons why real estate is made-to-order excitement. No other form of investment allows the small investor to get involved so easily and with so little money. No other form maximizes the laws of leverage for income, growth, and tax write-offs. There are many other reasons, but permeating them all is that you have control over your investments.

I've spent a lot of time comparing the benefits of real estate investing to other forms of investments. I think you can guess that I'm excited about real estate, and I get even more excited as I travel and meet with people who are also excited. Nobody ever comes up and shows me what their corporate stock is doing. One person, though, was excited about the ups and downs of the gold market. Apparently, he bought gold at $600 an ounce, just before it went to $800. That is exciting, but guess what? He forgot to sell it before it went to $300. Now he's playing the waiting game—totally out of control.

Over half of the people I teach are paying no taxes because of real estate tax write-offs. The others are on their way to doing the same. At least one third were working full time less than a year before (from the time I asked them this) and now are investing in real estate full time. Not only are they in control of their investments, but of their time as well. Most of them are on their way to being millionaires—looking forward to a great retirement.

If this sort of thing were happening to only a few people every now and then, I would say it was luck or a fluke or something. But it's happening to rich and poor alike, and it's happening everywhere. It puts a lot of fun into teaching because there are so many fun things to teach!

The Need To Improve

Every one of us has a need to improve. This is not something that I'm preaching, but something that I've observed. People want to be better off tomorrow than they are today. It's downright exciting when we know that we are growing.

It's fun to set and achieve goals. If we want to grow each year, we can map out the strategy to do so. A little hard work and we're there.

One man I know was a part-time Boy Scout leader. He wanted to give all of his time to it. After two years of part-time investing, he quit his job and is now a regional director for the

Boy Scouts. He's still buying and fixing up houses once in a while, and guess who does some of the fix-up? That's right–his troops.

Real estate gives us unlimited opportunities to learn new things, from law to fixing roofs, from title reports to values, from landlording to taxes. Every day is a college course.

At first, investing is scary. I was as nervous as a turkey in November with my first few houses. However, that feeling passed with experience. Soon I was moving in and out of houses with speed, determination, and knowledge. You will too, as you invest. You'll notice that I use the word "as." You have to actually work at it to get better. There are no substitutes for on-the-job training.

Real estate allows us not only to improve financially but personally as well. Investing is a kind of character test—to find out if we have any character, or if we're just a character. We need to improve, but no amount of improvement means anything unless we can measure it.

Measurability

I've mentioned this before, but it has a special meaning for this chapter. Yes, we can measure other forms of investments, and, like them, real estate can be measured. There are standard accepted ways to put values on real estate. If we hold a note, it can be measured to the penny. If we have a rental unit, there are ratios and comparables to help establish values.

There are easy ways to measure returns and yields to see how well our money (or equity) is performing. Because all of these things are measurable, it is usually quite simple to liquidate our holdings. There are literally thousands and thousands of people who put a high demand on real estate, its measurability and usability.

All of these yardsticks make real estate as good an investment as any other—until leveraged results are figured in, and then real estate zooms out ahead and doesn't look back.

Day To Day

I don't know too many people who want to be active in the day-to-day affairs of real estate investing for the rest of their lives. Most use real estate as a means to an end. That's the way it should be, but it's necessary at first to put in the long hours and go through the grind.

Can that be fun? Before I answer that, let me explain my personal definition of fun: it's slapping my knee and stomping my foot because I just took a couple of properties off the bank's hands—properties that were sitting and rotting in their REO file. Fun is at least 30 minutes of carrying on because the properties were 30% below market.

My idea of fun is a weekend in the mountains when I turn three properties in one week. I even get excited and have a party every time I assume a loan with an interest rate below 7%.

I once sent a box of chocolates to each of 18 tenants after I had finally devised a way for them to pay their rents on time, and they came through for me. I like to smile and enjoy my free time. That's fun to me—and real estate gives me more than I can handle.

What about the problems? They're no fun until they are taken care of. Then they are twice as much fun.

Now, let's explore why real estate is fun every day. You'll read elsewhere about running your investments like a business. You'll learn a lot about the things you'll need to do to accomplish this. Can these things be fun? If your attitude is right, it can be terribly exciting.

You'll be looking at new properties, talking with real estate agents, and exploring possibilities. You'll be placing ads in newspapers and meeting with contractors. Then you'll be hopping down to the title company to read over the final documents. A tenant will call to tell you about tire tracks that were imbedded deep in the front lawn from a drunken driver the night before. You'll cancel an appointment and drive like crazy to track down a foreclosure you just heard about. At 4:00 PM the title company will call to tell you that it will be another four days until they can close on the Bennett Street house. That means that the funds that you will need to fix up the Montgomery Avenue house are held up. You'll just have to put off the contractor and tenants another week. At 5:00 PM you remember that you forgot to return the carpet shampooer to Alpha Beta, and you'll have to pay another day's rent. 5:30 PM rolls around and your wife calls for you to bring home a bucket of chicken. Good, that will give you time to drive by three houses and a duplex for sale over by the mall.

Nobody has written or can write a book telling you what you'll do on any given day. The next day you may be up early to reconsider buying the house that a man called to tell you about while you were eating your last piece of chicken the night before. It's vacant and the back door is open, so you scoot over there before the buses even start running. Perhaps it could be turned into a good deal after all. By the time you're through, morning rush hour traffic has started, and it takes you longer to get back than anticipated. You're now running late, but that's okay. It's your time. You won't do anything today that resembles what you did yesterday. There are no clones in this business—just a lot of activity that seems to get out of control sometimes. Activity breeds activity. Once you start the ball rolling—once you plant the seeds—it's hard to slow down.

Can you find fun and happiness in all of this? I know thousands of people who have. Why? Because it's their time, their money, their properties that they're working with; and nobody does as good a job with your assets as you will. Doing a good job is the most fun of all.

Stay Motivated

Sometimes you may be forced to stay motivated. The sheer urgency of a problem makes it mandatory that you act. But putting problems aside, the daily routine is fun because it keeps us busy—busy heading somewhere while maintaining our control. Being busy is better than being bored.

Motivation can and should come from within. Sometimes, though, we need a little help. Maybe our successes will help. I was on cloud nine for three weeks after assuming a $14,800 note and mortgage at a 4¹/₄% interest rate. I couldn't sleep one night after tracking down and tying up a home that was being foreclosed on. It was valued in the $60,000 price range, and I got it for $12,000 with $1,800 due in back payments.

This sort of thing happens all the time. I guess you realize that it won't happen to you unless you're on the street trying to make it happen (or have someone there making it happen for you). Believe me, it is enjoyable, and I invite you to put out the effort and find out for yourself.

Another source of help that investors have is other investors and agents. Local people, national speakers who come to town, and others can create excitement. They can get the blood pumping again and teach you new techniques.

Associate With Successful People.

Be around them to get motivated or to get educated—maybe you need both. I know a young couple in Miami who spent $5,200 in one year traveling the country attending seminars. When they returned home, though, they purchased over $1.5 million of real estate. Does it really matter why they went? They gained the information and motivation to be doers, not dreamers. And just think, you can travel to your favorite places, or any place you've wanted to visit and use the expense as a tax write-off.

Fun To Watch

Most real estate investors I know really enjoy seeing their financial statements. It's a thrill to see yourself growing. If you invest right, this growth can mean a lot of income.

It's also fun to see individual properties go through the fixing-up process. Perhaps you bought a property and sold it as a good deal to someone else. They were people who couldn't qualify for a bank loan because they hadn't been on their present job for two years. You're their only hope for owning a home. They go to work fixing it up, and then, at the worst possible time, two years later, they sell it and pay off their note to you. Now you have $23,000 cash and need to buy other properties to create more tax shelters.

It's a never-ending cycle. Every day you'll be working with people. Sometimes people can drag you down, but if your attitude is right, these relationships can be quite enjoyable.

You'll never lack excitement. Running a real estate investment company is the most exciting thing you can ever do. If you're like me, everything else is boring by comparison.

Even if you're not an actual corporation, you still own one hundred percent stock in you. You're the chairman of the board, the CEO, and the dishwasher. If you want to invest in the stock market, invest in your own stock. Invest in your gray matter and go for the gold medal. The race is yours: run it well.

As A Business

When any investment plan is considered, we need to look at the aspects that will help it to continue to be a success. It's relatively easy to make a one-time killing in any investment, but how do we duplicate it? How do we make the same thing happen time and time again and even use our successes and failures as a foundation for future growth and success?

The way to do this is to treat the investment as a business. Realize it has obligations and features like any other business. Real estate offers a great advantage over other forms of investment, and all of the things I've mentioned so far in this book can be put to work in a business format. If done, your business of real estate will stand a much better chance of success. As a matter of fact, every other area of your life will be better.

Why is it important to run your investment like a business? Because businesses are forced to do certain things. Consider some of the aspects we've mentioned so far:

- Use of the law of leverage
- Tax planning
- Planning for equity growth
- Future obligations and opportunities
- Retirement

- Creation of cash flow

- Hiring employees or contractors

- Goal planning and review

- Using outside forces and measurements

- Education—books and seminars to keep improving

- Insurance and assurance planning

- Taking advantage of daily chores to build income and growth

- Fixing up and improving properties and neighborhoods

- Establishing a team of professionals

And the list goes on and on. Would a business in any other field have to do these things? Obviously, yes. And doing them well makes the plan click.

You, As President

I've told people to treat themselves like corporate executives. The board of directors and CEO of a company do certain things to make the company prosper, but they also like to play golf. It's important not only to have the right mixture of the things mentioned before, but to have the right mixture of your time.

To create this right mixture, we set priorities. That's good, but let me add one thing here. Priorities and goal planning are vital, but as soon as you think you have it all figured out, something happens to change everything. A deal falls through or an unexpected great property comes along. Many times my dedication was to whatever was urgent at the time. This is okay. Every business is like that. It is necessary to float to solve and end each problem as it arises because no one else can do it the way we can.

Sometimes we have to do things we don't like to do. If we can make the unenjoyable enjoyable, so much the better. As with any business, the routine things done right breed success.

Business Concepts

One of the most important concepts a business must learn is to decide whether or not to build a better mousetrap. There is no reason for us to continually reinvent the wheel. You can add a spoke here or there, or get a new tire when it is needed, but it isn't always necessary to actually create a new wheel or game plan.

Other people have pioneered systems and approaches, and they are more than willing to share their knowledge with us. Let's use them and their ideas to the fullest.

I heard a story several years ago about a mousetrap company that actually tried to build a better mousetrap. They figured they could make it cheaper and sell it for less, and their new plastic model would be much more efficient—saving the mouse a lot of pain.

It came out at ten cents when the old wooden ones were selling for fifteen cents, and it was a pretty plastic. They had high expectations of the world beating a path to their "mousehold" door. However, instead of turning into the big cheese of the mousetrap industry, which would surely have incurred the wrath of Disney fans everywhere, the trap was a dismal failure.

It seems that because the traps were so nice people wanted to keep them. That presented a problem. Usually, someone's wife would have had to open up the trap to discard the mutilated mouse, and that was a gruesome chore. Previously, the wife would just throw the whole thing away—mousetrap, mouse, and all. Now she would let the matter reside in a corner of the kitchen until the husband came home to do it. Then the trap would sit on a shelf forever waiting until the next time, or so the company thought. The next time a mouse came around, the wife bought and used the old wooden ones because the new plastic ones were too good to use.

So once we've tried and tested different investment ideas, it's time to stick to our guns. The biggest mistakes I've ever made were ones made when I stopped doing the successful things I had been doing. I developed the system of thinking big in many small ways. Everything went fine until I tried to invent a new wheel to roll in a different direction.

Back To Basics—The Four P's

What I'm going to reiterate now is right out of Business 101, but this information is pertinent and necessary to our investment business.

The four P's of running a business are:

1. Planning

2. Production

3. Promotion

4. Placement

These aspects of business are all necessary. Fail to do one and you court disaster. You see, many people know that they have a good idea, but they don't produce it the right way—and it fails. Perhaps it did get produced correctly, but there wasn't an adequate placement or delivery system. It's sad to see good ideas and products fail because all four "P's" are not intact.

1. Planning: we've spent adequate time in the first few chapters explaining what real estate can do. We'll stay a step ahead by knowing what we want out of our investment. Once we determine our goal in terms of growth, income, and tax savings, then we can plan which properties to buy, hold, and sell. To fail to plan is to plan to fail. Yes, that saying is trite and true, but sometimes these phrases are the best way to make a point.

2. Production: treat properties like inventory. Once you know your goal, stockpile the necessary inventory. You'll need to watch your inventory, the way any business does. Floor space is valuable. We all need to maximize our efforts to gain the most production possible. It may be hard at first, but we, like a business, need to quickly get working to full production. This is the area where we accomplish the most if we can get a team of professionals to produce the most.

3. Promotion: this area includes advertising and almost everything else that moves one's ideas. I use the word *ideas* because once the plan is set and we know what production is needed, we have to set in motion the machine to accomplish our purposes. Remember, if we don't, nobody else will.

The better we are at promoting our properties, the sooner we can go on to bigger and better things. Getting on is the key to success. Let's not ever minimize the importance of promotion.

4. Placement: this aspect involves settling an affair. If we are selling kites, placement would involve putting them in toy stores. In real estate we're talking about actually renting or selling the property. Placement, though, is most effective, as you can well guess, when it's in harmony with the three other P's and sees that they outperform our original expectations.

Placement is the act that frees up our time and money to get on. It is not just an integral part but the P that the other three P's are working for. We should understand and be ready to exercise this P before we ever get involved.

Summary
I hope this little review will help you see ways to tighten up your investments. In an economy such as the current one, we need an edge. We need to run our investments like a business.

There's no room for inefficiency. It is mandatory that we build cautiously and slowly. Honesty is by far the best policy. There's so little competition.

I almost want to dare you to run your investments like a business, with all the care, concern, hard work, and thinking that a business requires—and then fail. Just try it. If you plant good seeds, you bear good fruit.

The biggest secret of being successful is that there are no secrets. Successful principles are universal and ready and willing and waiting to go to work for you. The principle that has meant the most to me (besides the teachings of my church) is to keep doing the things that have made me successful. Be repetitious. Use the football play to get the touchdown that you have been using to get you down the field. In short, dance with the girl you brought to the dance.

AVAILABLE RESOURCES

The following books, videos, and audiocassettes have been reviewed by the Wade Cook Seminars, Inc. or Lighthouse Publishing Group, Inc. staff and are suggested as reading and resource material for continuing education to help with your financial planning, and real estate and stock market investments. Because new ideas and techniques come along and laws change, we're always updating our catalogue.

To order a copy of our current catalogue, please write or call us at:

Wade Cook Seminars, Inc.
14675 Interurban Avenue South
Seattle, Washington 98168-4664
1–800–872–7411

Or, visit us on our web sites at:

www.wadecook.com
www.lighthousebooks.com

Also, we would love to hear your comments on our products and services, as well as your testimonials on how these products have benefited you. We look forward to hearing from you!

Stock Market

Income Formulas—A free cassette
By Wade B. Cook

Learn the 11 cash flow formulas taught in the Wall Street Workshop. Learn to double some of your money in 2½ to 4 months.

Wall Street Money Machine
By Wade B. Cook

Appearing on the *New York Times* Business Best Sellers list for over one year, **Wall Street Money Machine** contains the best strategies for wealth enhancement and cash flow creation you'll find anywhere. Throughout this book, Wade Cook describes many of his favorite strategies for generating cash flow through the stock market: Rolling Stock, Proxy Investing, Covered Calls, and many more. It's a great introduction for creating wealth using the Wade Cook formulas.

Stock Market Miracles
By Wade B. Cook

The anxiously-awaited partner to **Wall Street Money Machine**, this book is proven to be just as invaluable. **Stock Market Miracles** improves on some of the strategies from **Wall Street Money Machine**, as well as introducing new and valuable twists on our old favorites. This is a must read for anyone interested in making serious money in the stock market.

Bear Market Baloney
By Wade B. Cook

A more timely book wouldn't be possible. Wade's predictions came true while the book was at press! Don't miss this insightful look into what makes bull and bear markets and how to make exponential returns in any market.

Dynamic Dollars Video
By Wade B. Cook

Wade Cook's 90 minute introduction to the basics of his Wall Street formulas and strategies. In this presentation designed especially for video, Wade explains the meter drop philosophy,

Rolling Stock, basics of Proxy Investing, and Writing Covered Calls. Perfect for anyone looking for a little basic information.

Zero To Zillions
By Wade B. Cook

This is a powerful audio workshop on Wall Street—understanding the stock market game, playing it successfully, and retiring rich. Learn eleven powerful investment strategies to avoid pitfalls and losses, catch "day-trippers," "bottom fish," write Covered Calls, double your money in one week on options on stock split companies, and so much more. Wade "Meter Drop" Cook will teach you how he makes fantastic annual returns in your account.

The Wall Street Workshop Video Series
By Wade B. Cook

If you can't make it to the Wall Street Workshop soon, get a head start with these videos. Ten albums containing eleven hours of intense instruction on Rolling Stock, options on stock split companies, writing Covered Calls, and eight other tested and proven strategies designed to help you increase the value of your investments. By learning, reviewing, and implementing the strategies taught here, you will gain the knowledge and the confidence to take control of your investments, and get your money to work hard for you.

The Next Step Video Series
By Team Wall Street

The advanced version of the Wall Street Workshop. Full of power-packed strategies from Wade Cook, this is not a duplicate of the Wall Street Workshop, but a very important partner. The methods taught in this seminar will supercharge the strategies taught in the Wall Street Workshop and teach you even more ways to make more money!

In the Next Step, you'll learn how to find the stocks to fit the formulas through technical analysis, fundamentals, home trading tools, and more.

Wealth Information Network (WIN)

This subscription computer bulletin board service provides you with the latest financial formulas and updated entity structuring strategies. New, timely information is entered Monday through Friday, sometimes four or five times a day. Wade Cook and his Team Wall Street staff write for WIN, giving you updates on their own current stock plays, companies who announced earnings, companies who announced stock splits, and the latest trends in the market.

WIN is also divided into categories according to specific strategies and contains archives of all our trades so you can view our history. If you are just getting started in the stock market, this is a great way to follow people who are doubling their money every $2^1/_2$ to 4 months. If you are experienced already, it's the way to confirm your feelings and research with others who are generating wealth through the stock market.

IQ Pager

This is a system which beeps you as events and announcements are made on Wall Street. With **IQ Pager**, you'll receive information about events like major stock split announcements, earnings surprises, important mergers and acquisitions, judgements or court decisions involving big companies, important bankruptcy announcements, big winners and losers, and disasters.   If you're getting your financial information from the evening news, you're getting it too late.   The key to the stock market is timing. Especially when you're trading in options, you need up-to-the-minute (or second) information. You cannot afford to sit at a computer all day looking for news or wait for your broker to call. **IQ Pager** is the ideal partner to the Wealth Information Network (WIN).

Entity Integration

Power Of Nevada Corporations—A free cassette
By Wade B. Cook

Nevada Corporations have secrecy, privacy, minimal taxes, no reciprocity with the IRS, and protection for shareholders, officers, and directors. This is a powerful seminar.

The Incorporation Handbook
By Wade B. Cook

Incorporation made easy! This handbook tells you who, why, and, most importantly, how to incorporate. Included are samples of the forms you will use when you incorporate, as well as a step-by-step guide from the experts.

The Financial Fortress Home Study Course
By Wade B. Cook

This eight-part series is the last word in entity structuring. It goes far beyond mere financial planning or estate planning, and helps you structure your business and your affairs so that you can avoid the majority of taxes, retire rich, escape lawsuits, bequeath your assets to your heirs without government interference, and, in short—bomb proof your entire estate. There are six audio cassette seminars on tape, an entity structuring video, and a full kit of documents.

Business Entity Skills Training (BEST)
Presented by Wade B. Cook and Team Wall Street

Learn about the six powerful entities you can use to protect your wealth and your family. Learn the secrets of asset protection, eliminate your fear of litigation, and minimize your taxes.

Real Estate

Income Streams—A free cassette
By Wade B. Cook

Learn to buy and sell real estate the Wade Cook way. This informative cassette will instruct you in building and operating your own real estate money machine.

Real Estate Money Machine
By Wade B. Cook

Wade's first bestselling book reveals the secrets of Wade Cook's own system—the system he earned his first million from. This book teaches you how to make money regardless of the state of the economy. Wade's innovative concepts for investing in real estate not only avoids high interest rates, but avoids banks altogether.

How To Pick Up Foreclosures
By Wade B. Cook

Do you want to become an expert money maker in real estate? This book will show you how to buy real estate at 60¢ on the dollar or less. You'll learn to find the house before the auction and purchase it with no bank financing—the easy way to millions in real estate. The market for foreclosures is a tremendous place to learn and prosper. *How To Pick Up Foreclosures* takes Wade's methods from *Real Estate Money Machine* and super charges them by applying the fantastic principles to already-discounted properties.

Owner Financing
By Wade B. Cook

This is a short but invaluable pamphlet you can give to sellers who hesitate to sell you their property using the owner financing method. Let this pamphlet convince both you and them. The special report, *"Why Sellers Should Take Monthly Payments,"* is included for free!

Real Estate For Real People
By Wade B. Cook

A priceless, comprehensive overview of real estate investing, this book teaches you how to buy the right property for the right price, at the right time. Wade Cook explains all of the strategies you'll need, and gives you 20 reasons why you should start investing in real estate today. Learn how to retire rich with real estate, and have fun doing it.

In With A Dime Out With A Dollar
By Wade B. Cook

Wade Cook has personally achieved success after success in real estate. *In With A Dime Out With A Dollar*, formerly 101 Ways To Buy Real Estate Without Cash fills the gap left by other authors who have given all the ingredients but not the whole recipe for real estate investing. This is the book for the investor who wants innovative and practical methods for buying real estate with little or no money down.

Legal Forms
By Wade B. Cook

This collection of pertinent forms contains numerous legal forms used in real estate transactions. These forms were selected by experienced investors, but are not intended to replace the advice of an attorney. However, they will provide essential forms for you to follow in your personal investing.

Record Keeping System
By Wade B. Cook

A complete record keeping system for organizing all of the information on each of your properties. This system keeps track of everything from insurance policies to equity growth. You will know at a glance exactly where you stand with your investment properties and you will sleep better at night.

Money Machine I & II
By Wade B. Cook

Learn the benefits of buying, and more importantly, selling real estate. Now the system for creating and maintaining a real estate money machine is available in audiocassette form. Money Machine I & II teach the step by step cash flow formulas that made Wade Cook and thousands like him millions.

Paper Tigers and Paper Chase
By Wade B. Cook

Wade gives you a personal introduction to the art of buying and selling real estate. In this set of six cassettes, Wade shares his inside secrets to establishing a cash flow business with real estate investments. You will learn how to find discounted second mortgages, find second mortgage notes and make them better, as well as how you can get 40%-plus yields on your money. Learn the art of structuring your business to attract investors and bring in the income you desire through the use of family corporations, pension plans, and other legal entities. A manual is included.

When you buy Paper Tigers, you'll also receive Paper Chase for free. Paper Chase holds the most important tools you need to make deals happen. Wade created these powerful tapes as a handout tool you can lend to potential investors or home owners to help educate them about how this amazing cash flow system works for them. It explains how you'll negotiate a lower interest rate if they make a larger payment. You will use this incredible tool over and over again.

Build Perpetual Income (BPI)—A videocassete

Wade Cook Seminars, Inc. is proud to present *Build Perpetual Income*, the latest in our ever-expanding series of seminar home study courses. In this video, you will learn powerful real estate cash-flow generating techniques, such as:

- Power negotiating strategies
- Buying and selling mortgages
- Writing contracts
- Finding and buying discount properties
- Avoiding debt

Assorted Financial Wisdom

Money Mysteries of the Millionaires—A free cassette
By Wade B. Cook

How to make money and keep it. This fantastic seminar shows you how to use Nevada Corporations, Living Trusts, Pension Plans, Business Trusts, Charitable Remainder Trusts, and Family Limited Partnerships to protect your assets.

Brilliant Deductions
By Wade B. Cook

Do you want to make the most of the money you earn? Do you want to have solid tax havens and ways to reduce the taxes you pay? This book is for you! Learn how to get rich in spite of the new tax laws. See new tax credits, year-end maneuvers, and methods for transferring and controlling your entities. Learn to structure yourself and your family for tax savings and liability protection. Available in bookstores or call our toll free number: 1-800-872-7411.

Blueprints for Success
1998
Contributors: Wade B. Cook, Keven Hart, Debbie Losse, Joel Black, Dan Wagner and Dave Wagner

Blueprints For Success is a compilation of chapters on building your wealth through your business and making your business function successfully. The chapters cover: education and information gathering, choosing the best business for you from all the different types of business, and a variety of other skills necessary for becoming successful. Your business can't afford to miss out on these powerful insights!

High Performance Business Strategies
By Wade B. Cook

Your business cannot succeed without you. This course will help *you* become successful so your company can succeed. It is a combination of two previous courses, formerly entitled Turbo-Charge Your Business and High-Octane Business Strategies. For years, Wade Cook and his staff have listened to people's questions, and concerns. Because they know that problems are best solved by people who already know the ropes, Wade's staff wanted to help. They categorized the questions and came up with about 60 major areas of concern. Wade then went into the recording studio and dealt head on with these questions. What resulted is a comprehensive collection of knowledge to get you started quickly.

Wealth 101 (1998)
By Wade B. Cook

This incredible book brings you 101 strategies for wealth creation and protection that you can't afford to miss. Front to back, it is packed full of tips and tricks to supercharge your financial health. If you need to generate more cash flow, this book shows you how through several various avenues. If you are already wealthy, this is the book that will show you strategy upon strategy for decreasing your tax liability and increasing your peace of mind through liability protection.

Unlimited Wealth Audio Set
By Wade B. Cook

Unlimited Wealth is the "University of Money-Making Ideas" home study course that helps you improve your money's personality. The heart and soul of this seminar is to make more money, pay fewer taxes, and keep more for your retirement and family. This cassette series contains the great ideas from **Wealth 101** on tape, so you can listen to them whenever you want.

Retirement Prosperity
By Wade B. Cook

Take that IRA money now sitting idle and invest it in ways that generate you bigger, better, and quicker returns. This four audiotape set walks you through a system of using a self directed IRA to create phenomenal profits, virtually tax free! This is one of the most complete systems for IRA investing ever created.

Travel Agent Information
By John Childers and Wade Cook

The only sensible solution for the frequent traveller. This kit includes all of the information and training you need to be an outside travel agent for a stable company. There are no hassles, no requirements, no forms or restriction, just all the benefits of travelling for substantially less *every time*.

Cook University

People enroll in **Cook University** for a variety of reasons. Usually they are a little discontented with where they are—their job is not working, their business is not producing the kind of income they want, or they definitely see that they need more income to prepare for a better retirement. That's where **Cook University** comes in. As you try to live the American Dream, in the life-style you want, we stand by ready to assist you make the dream your reality.

The backbone of the one-year program is the Money Machine concept—as applied to your business, to stock investments, or to real estate. Although there are many, many other forms of investing in real estate, there are really only three that work: the Money Machine method, buying second mortgages, and lease options. Of these three, the Money Machine stands head and shoulders above the rest:

It is difficult to explain *Cook University* in only a few words. It is so unique, innovative and creative that it literally stands alone. But then, what would you expect from Wade Cook? Something common and ordinary? Never! Wade and his staff always go out of their way to provide you with useful, tried-and-true strategies that create real wealth.

We are embarking on an unprecedented voyage and want you to come along. If you choose to make this important decision in your life, you could also be invited to share your successes in a series of books called *Blueprints For Success* (*more volumes to come*). Yes, it takes commitment. Yes, it takes drive. Add to this the help you'll receive by our hand-trained experts and you will enhance your asset base and increase your bottom line.

We want to encourage a lot of people to get in the program right away. You could save thousands of dollars, if you don't delay. Call right away! Class sizes are limited so each student gets personal attention.

Perpetual monthly income is waiting. We'll teach you how to achieve it. We'll show you how to make it. We'll watch over you while you're making it happen. Thank you for your consideration. We hope to see you in the program right away.

Cook University is designed to be an integral part of your educational life. We encourage you to call and find out more about this life–changing program. The number is 1–800–872–7411. Ask for an enrollment director and begin your millionaire-training today!

If you want to be wealthy, this is the place to be.

Classes Offered:

The Wall Street Workshop
Presented by Wade B. Cook and Team Wall Street

The Wall Street Workshop teaches you how to make incredible money in all markets. It teaches you the tried-and-true strategies that have made hundreds of people wealthy.

The Next Step Workshop
Presented by Wade B. Cook and Team Wall Street

An Advanced Wall Street Workshop designed to help those ready to take their trading to the next level and treat it as a business. This seminar is open only to graduates of the Wall Street Workshop.

Executive Retreat
Presented by Wade B. Cook and Team Wall Street

Created especially for the individuals already owning or planning to establish Nevada Corporations, the Executive Retreat is a unique opportunity for corporate executives to participate in workshops geared toward streamlining operations and maximizing efficiency and impact.

Wealth Academy
Presented by Wade B. Cook and Team Wall Street

This three day workshop defines the art of asset protection and entity planning. During these three days we will discuss, in depth and detail, the six domestic entities which will protect you from lawsuits, taxes, or other financial losses, and help you retire rich.

Real Estate Workshop
Presented by Wade B. Cook and Team Main Street

The Real Estate Workshop teaches you how to build perpetual income for life, without going to work. Some of the topics include buying and selling paper, finding discounted properties, generating long-term monthly cash flow, and controlling properties wihtout owning them.

Real Estate Bootcamp
Presented by Wade B. Cook and Team Main Street

This three to four day Bootcamp is truly a roll-up-your-sleeves-and-do-the-deals event. You will be learning how to locate the bargains, negotiate strategies, and find wholesale properties (pre-foreclosures). You will also visit a title company, look at properties and learn some new and fun selling strategies.

PROPERTY ANALYSIS FORM

Property Address _____ Person in Charge _____

Type of Property_____ Owner _____ Phone _____

Describe _____

_____

Zoning _____ Chance for change?_____

How long has property been for sale? _____

What is original asking price? _____

Adjustments to price _____ Date _____ , _____ Date _____

What is owner willing to take? Explain _____

_____

EXISTING FINANCING

	Loan 1	Loan 2	Loan 3	Loan 4
Lender				
Balance				
Payment				
Int. rate				
Pymt includes				
Assumable?				
Explain				

OWNER'S EQUITY

How much equity does owner have?_____

How much down do they want? _____ When do they need it?_____

Are they willing to carry any on a note? _____How much? _____

What interest rate?_____Payment? _____

Alternatives to finance the down payment: _____

Alternatives to finance the balance of owner's equity:_____

_____

What is owner willing to fix? _____

RENT

Unit 1 _____ Unit 2 _____ Unit 3 _____

Unit 4 _____ Unit 5 _____ Unit 6 _____

Total rents now _____ When? _____

Explain _____

AGENT/COMMISSION

Is there: an agent? _____ commission? _____

How is agent willing to take his commission? _____

FIX-UP

Estimated fix-up costs _____

What needs fixing up? _____

_____

Value after fix-up _____

SCENARIO

	#1	#2	#3
Purchase Price			
Fix-Up			
Sell price			
Profit			
Explain			

RECOMMENDATION

Purchase offer _____

_____

_____

_____

Use _____

_____

_____

_____